How to
Set Up Your Own
Neighborhood Preschool

How to
Set Up Your Own
Neighborhood Preschool

Ruth Tucker and Kit Bernthal

Illustrated by Kit Bernthal

Book design by Pat Slesarchik

Manufactured in the United States of America

P 10 9 8 7 6 5 4 3 2 1

Library of Congress Cataloging in Publication Data

Tucker, Ruth, 1945–
  How to set up your own neighborhood preschool.

  Bibliography: p.
  Includes index.
  1. Education, Preschool—Handbooks, manuals,
etc.   2. Community schools—Handbooks, manuals,
etc.   3. Creative activities and seat work—
Handbooks, manuals, etc.   I. Bernthal, Kit,
1948–   joint author.   II. Title.
LB1140.2.T8   372.21   79-12123
ISBN 0-87000-432-8

For Carlton,
Chip, Jason, Jeff,
and Matthew

Contents

Part Two: Challenging the Child

Part One

Preparing the Parent

1

That Crucial Year

Deciding whether or not to send your child to nursery school is a dilemma that you may be facing. Though the number of preschools in this country has risen dramatically in recent years, many parents are still keeping their children at home. If you are one of these parents, perhaps you are discouraged by the high cost of modern nursery-school education. Even if you can afford the tuition and are able to find a quality school near your home, you may seriously doubt whether your child is ready to start school at the tender age of three or four. Little ones grow up so fast, and sending them off to school at such an early age may seem to be rushing things.

As a mother who is home with her preschooler, you experience many rewarding moments, moments made more precious by their fleeting nature. If you are in tune with your youngster during these sensitive years you can learn much from him and can teach him much in return. Never again will you have a chance to be as close to your child as in these years before kindergarten. For after you relinquish him to his first teacher, most of his days will be spent in the care of another adult. In most cases, you will have little say about what your child does or about who guides him during these school years.

Yet, to be candid, the years when mother and child are home together are not perfect bliss. There are times when a preschooler's constant cheerful chatter can be unnerving to even the most patient of mothers. There are times, too, when tripping over toys and sponging up puddles on the kitchen floor becomes too much to handle gracefully. Every mother needs some free time to spend with pet projects, younger children, housework, or just relaxing. Every youngster needs playmates.

13

Also, a child's first school experience will be easier if he has already worked and played with children his own age, and is able to relax when his mother leaves him in the care of another adult. Most three-year-olds would benefit socially, physically, and mentally from a "head start."

What, then, is the ideal situation for both mother and child? In answering this question we considered what we wanted for ourselves and our children. First, we wanted to preserve our close contact with our preschoolers. Second, we wanted them to have a small group of friends to play and learn with. Third, we preferred to have a structured situation where free play would alternate with activities for social, physical, and mental development. Ideally, this situation would provide some free time for us and be as inexpensive as possible. The home nursery school emerged as the answer to our needs.

In our group, we had five mothers and five three-year-old boys: Matthew, Carlton, Jeff, Jason, and Chip. We decided that each mother should take the children into her home on Monday, Wednesday, and Friday mornings for a week. For the four following weeks she would take her child to another mother's home. We were happy to see that when our school was in full swing, the boys enjoyed themselves. We enjoyed ourselves. The boys learned more about themselves, other people, and their environment than we ever could have taught them on an individual basis. And, instead of costing us money for tuition, the plan resulted in profits for the mothers: free time, meaningful teaching, and peace of mind.

We had created a steppingstone between home and formal schooling which proved to be an ideal arrangement for our little ones. The children felt a sense of security that reassured their families. Carlton, having just turned three, perhaps expressed this feeling most pointedly: the prospect of going to school at a "building" with "teachers" seemed a bit overwhelming, but going to "houses" with "mommies" was just right.

What Should Preschoolers Learn?

Especially appealing to us was the idea of deciding for ourselves what was most important for our children to learn. In order for our nursery school to have a positive impact on our children, we set up the following priorities.

14

First, each child should enjoy himself. This was not the only reason our nursery school existed, but the success of the rest of our goals depended on the first one. We felt free to interrupt a "lesson" that was becoming stale for a romp in the leaves before returning to crayons and paper.

Second, each child should have the opportunity to discover his own identity. He should see himself positively in situations involving both real life and future goals. "I'm a good helper with the name tags today," Matthew said proudly, "and when I get bigger, I can write the names on, too."

Not only should each youngster know such personal information as his full name, address, and telephone number, but he should also realize his potential and his real value to friends, strangers, and family. As he is discovering his own identity, the child comes to appreciate other people. He begins to see the importance and consequences of his actions in relationship to his own "little society." Chip had to spend some time in the hospital while his tonsils and adenoids were removed. When the nurse asked him if he was going to tell his brothers and sisters what happened to him, he responded, "I don't have any brothers and sisters. I'm going to tell the nursery-school kids." Because Chip was an only child, he needed to be part of a social group. He was important to them, and they would gladly share his experiences.

While a child develops socially in relating to his peers, he also learns to accept outside authority. We found that the children became very fond of the mothers in authority. Their influence was felt even outside of nursery school. "Why can't I jump on the furniture, Mom? Because Mrs. Tucker says so?" The children can become personally attached to the mother of a friend, besides having respect for her as a teacher. We found this to be true in our group, and it wasn't uncommon to hear, "Let's pretend that I'm Matthew and you're Mrs. Bernthal. Okay, Mom?"

In addition to understanding himself and relating to others, a child should begin to discover the world around him. He should see himself in relationship to nature, animals, seasons, and time. He should see his role in perspective to his environment through nature hikes, field trips, and planned crafts and readings. For example, though youngsters should be taught the dangers of venturing alone into a large body of water, they should also see that water can help them care for their little

15

vegetable gardens. They will like the idea of being able to help things grow. A sense of responsibility for natural beauty developed at this age will help them to have a greater concern for the environment as they grow older.

Physical development is also important. When the child develops finger coordination, he can do more things for himself and, therefore, become more independent. Stringing beads in nursery school soon leads a child to lacing his own shoes. The stronger and more coordinated a child becomes, the more easily he can join in games with his neighborhood and school friends.

In addition, a child should progress mentally, by developing reasoning powers, learning to recognize likenesses and differences, and sharpening the senses. He may also be introduced to such reading and academic readiness skills as recognition of alphabet letters, numbers, sizes, and shapes. But these studies should never be frustrating to the child or interfere with his ability to appreciate his own beauty and the beauty of his world.

By placing personal enjoyment first, we tried to treat the three-year-olds first as small children and only second as students. Since the priorities overlapped, many activities served to develop the children in all areas of concern. And, as we watched them have fun learning, we felt that the benefits they reaped could not have been garnered if they had stayed at home by themselves.

What Are the Benefits of the Group Situation?

While a firm parental foundation at home prepares children for the future, a youngster needs outside group experience to become a well-rounded person. Independence, for instance, was encouraged by our home nursery school; the children were neither placed in totally unfamiliar surroundings nor completely sheltered from the outside world. Since each child was not home all the time, he had to accept another adult's authority. He had to rely on himself to see that he accomplished his toilet duties, kept his possessions intact, identified his own coat and hat, and received his share of attention and toys. He served himself snacks, set the table, and cleaned up after play. The most coveted tasks were passing out napkins and turning pages while mother read the story for the day. If a child had previously depended on his mother to dress him, he began to insist on putting on his own coat after seeing that the others could. If he had formerly relied on mom's help in coloring a picture, he now felt proud to show his friends he could do it himself.

Each child had an opportunity to develop leadership qualities by being "in charge" of activities at his own house. He passed out name tags, toys, and craft items. He delegated authority in ringing the school bell and in leading games or exercises. These benefits far exceeded any growth opportunities the child might have had at home.

Furthermore, each youngster was allowed to explore his own feelings and skills in relationship to those outside the home environment. Matthew, who was angry at his baby brother, was surprised that Chip thought he was lucky to have a younger sibling. Jason and Jeff discovered unknown talents when together they built a spaceship from Tinkertoys. A child who previously had not paid attention to colors, shapes, or numbers regarded them with more interest if his friends were learning them. If he wasn't interested in hygiene or cleanliness, he was exposed to children who blew their own noses, washed their hands and faces, and brushed leaves from their sweaters before entering the house.

In short, the youngsters learned to share, to give and take in group situations, and to respect individual differences. They learned to cooperate, to rely on themselves, and to believe in their own abilities.

What Benefits Might the Families Expect?

The mothers in our group also gained from the home nursery school. Free time was an unaccustomed pleasure; during the four weeks when the other mothers held school, each of us was able to relax, catch up on reading or hobbies, and get other work done, enabling us to spend more free time with our boys when they got home. Personal projects were accomplished unhindered, and siblings enjoyed some moments of private contact with mother. Jeff's older brother, who came home from kindergarten an hour before Jeff returned, enjoyed the special time with his mother; and on days when school was at Jeff's house, he was mom's helper. Matthew's younger brother enjoyed his morning with mother and his big brother's toys, but was always happy to greet Matthew at the door when he came home. By noon, the mothers were prepared to greet the little ones and admire the "treasures" they brought home in their school bags. Jeff sat in a special chair when he showed his mother the things he had made.

Each of the families involved felt the effect of the boys' program. School and home life were closely integrated. The boys were not just class members, but vital, functioning members of a miniature society. The feelings they developed for each other reached beyond nursery school to home and neighborhood associations. When the nurse in the hospital asked Chip if he had any allergies, he replied, "Penicillin, and Jason can't have milk"—he had to watch out for Jason's well-being even when he wasn't in school. After Matthew learned to play "London Bridge" at Jeff's house, he took more interest in his baby brother, because he wanted him to play the game with him. Matthew also became less worried about protecting his own possessions and more concerned about having fun through cooperative playing.

Since they were not surrounded by the same play situation for all their waking hours, the children made better use of their time at home. They didn't have to rely on television for stimulation. Instead of the "TV squat," they learned the bunny hop. And they made interesting contributions to family conversation. Matthew, who had previously paid little attention to the change of seasons, showed new interest after having been to school. When his mother was getting ready to shovel snow off the front walk, she asked him if he wanted to join her. "No, Mom," he replied, "the snow's gonna shovel itself. Mrs. Kleine says that when it's warm, the snow goes away."

Perhaps the greatest joy shared by all of the mothers was the actual teaching of their own preschool sessions. We found it tremendously satisfying to witness the different personalities interact. The shy boys relaxed and joined in the fun; the quiet ones forgot themselves and squealed with excitement; the aggressive ones channeled their leadership desires by passing out toys; and all of them genuinely enjoyed each other's company. The boys were not always perfect angels, but we learned to deal with discipline problems on an individual basis.

In short, teaching the children did not become a chore, as

some might expect, but a rewarding challenge. And, mostly, it was fun. It gave us the chance to cut, paste, and color with the excuse that we were preparing to teach. We also experienced every teacher's satisfaction in sharing something valuable with someone else. And the boys' attachment to the teachers meant we all had made valuable friendships, not only with the cooperating mothers but also with their children.

Though the children and their families benefited most from the home nursery school, there were also benefits for the neighborhood. An elderly widow shared an especially joyful experience. The five boys were taking a nature hike when they noticed her waving to them from her front porch. Carlton's mother took them up to the house to say hello, and they spent a few minutes talking and singing nursery rhymes for her. The laugh lines on her leathery cheeks and the enthusiastic flush of the boys' chubby ones told the story of a delightful encounter.

Why Not a Traditional Nursery School?

Enrolling a child in a traditional nursery school can provide some of the same advantages as did our home nursery school. However, for several reasons, we found this option much less desirable than our program.

By working at home, we saved money. Nursery schools in our area charge between $20 and $30 a month, and in urban areas average $40 to $60 a month. We did not want to spend $300 to $600 a year on a program we weren't enthusiastic about in the first place. Using a little imagination, we were able to design personalized activities adapted to our own children's abilities for just the cost of materials. By scrounging, using scraps, or spending nominal fees on materials, we gave our children an enriched program for practically nothing. They enjoyed making egg-cup caterpillars and milk-carton bird feeders, and they discovered that they could make fun toys instead of purchasing them at a department store.

What if you can afford the tuition? Why not leave preschool education to the "experts"? We read about nursery schools, we visited them ourselves, and we found that they could not be considered expert. Further, we decided that we wanted to take a more active part in deciding how our children should grow in the impressionable preschool years.

The "experts" teaching children in our area often had no education past high school and none had recent training in preschool education. Even if they had been thoroughly trained, we felt that, when it came to our own children, mother was as much of an expert as most strangers. Five mothers, each with different talents and abilities and each having a close relationship with the children, could provide fresh approaches to learning. Because each of us was to be "on the job" only every fifth week, we believed that our enthusiasm could be easily maintained. Since we planned to operate on similar schedules each week, the children didn't have to adjust to totally different teaching approaches. And we had no problem with continuity, since we discussed our sessions periodically.

Children do not have to be in a classroom to learn to behave in school. If respecting others' rights and opinions means sometimes raising your hand or waiting your turn to answer, children can do this easily in a living room or even in a sandbox. When the boys were playing "Zoo Lotto," a matching card game, in the living room, some of them began grabbing for cards they thought belonged in their piles. Jeff, who was passing out cards at the time, held the cards away from them and calmly waited for each child to raise his hand before he received his card. Our three-year-olds' barely dry bottoms were more comfortable on the sofa than on a hard desk chair. In fact, the boys could more easily pay attention to their peers in a smaller group than in a class of fifteen. Games involving five children require more personal involvement and at least as much self-restraint as those involving fifteen children at once. A classmate's comment, such as "Jason's not making a bunny with his fingers," can bring forth a response from the child whose attention has temporarily wandered.

Our state (Indiana) provided no guidelines and standards for nursery schools. Even if it had, we would have been reluctant to entrust our little ones to strangers. A kindergartner could tell us if he felt isolated or threatened in a certain situation, but a three-year-old's awareness and communication skills are not as well-developed.

Since our children's physical health and safety were such a concern for us, we visited the nursery schools in our town to assess the situation. We were not pleased with what we found. According to John Goodlad's nationwide study of nursery schools, most states have no better control over their nursery schools than ours does.* When we tried to find out from each state what their policies were, we were not sure even where to write. Nursery schools, if acknowledged at all, were handled by different agencies in each state.

Nor are there any nationwide government or professional health, safety, and curriculum standards for nursery schools. Preschoolers, who are curious about everything, are virtually defenseless against some dangers such as fire and objects falling from carelessly stacked shelves. The younger children are, the fewer provisions there are to protect them. If we had sent our children to one of the traditional nursery schools that we investigated, we would have been releasing them into an uncontrolled situation.

In Indiana, day-care centers are closely regulated and inspected, but building inspection of nursery schools is practically nonexistent. Day-care centers are required to have at least one college-trained person designing a program for attending children, but nursery schools don't have to follow any requirements at all. It seems if children meet someplace for only two or three hours, what they do, or how unsafe they may be doesn't matter.

In our town we found six nursery schools. The existence and whereabouts of most of these was discovered only by word of mouth. When we visited them we evaluated them according to licensing standards for day-care centers.† Day-care centers are required to staff one adult for every ten to fifteen children. Most of the local nursery schools had similar ratios, but this class size seemed to work better for four-year-olds than for three-year-olds. One teacher, confronting fifteen three-year-

*John Goodlad, *Early Schooling in the United States* (New York: McGraw-Hill, 1973).

†Day-care center guideline and licensing references are available from: U.S. Department of Health, Education and Welfare, Office of Child Development, Bureau of Child Development Services, Washington, D.C. 20201 (request DHEW Publication No. [OCD] 73-1053); and Education Commission of the States, 300 Lincoln Tower, 1860 Lincoln Street, Denver, Colorado 80203 (request Report No. 72, Early Childhood Report # B).

olds for the first time, called the situation impossible. She had to have a mother come in to help at each session. We felt we could handle our five students better in case of emergency than anyone else could handle fifteen or twenty. Most schools did not even conduct fire drills, and their buildings could in no way be considered fireproof. The prospect of fifteen three-year-olds not knowing what to do or where to go in a smoking building frightened us.

If fire extinguishers were present on the schools' premises, most teachers did not know exactly where they were or how to use them. One school was conducted in the basement of a large, ranch-style home. There was only one exit, and this was up a flight of stairs. Another school occupied two small rooms in a very old home. The only unblocked exit opened inward, and children had to descend five steps to ground level outside, further adding to the danger of injury. The schools conducted in homes had had no recent fire inspection.

Health procedures outlined for day-care centers were not followed by most nursery schools. Snacks were provided to large groups of children daily, but procedures were not inspected by the local health department. Disposable cups, personalized utensils, or water fountains are recommended for day-care centers. Half the nursery schools used cups washed by hand. Most nursery schools didn't require teacher health exams, although day-care centers and even public schools require at least TB tests. Bathroom facilities were sometimes located on a floor other than the one the students were on. Four-year-olds might not mind this, but our youngsters' races to the bathroom made us wonder what would happen if four or five of them had to scramble upstairs at once. If a child had trouble, the teacher would have to leave her large group unsupervised.

With our own strict regulation and mutual inspection of our homes, as outlined in the next chapter, we were satisfied that our children were learning in a safe, clean environment.

Quivering chins and dewy eyes are three-year-old reactions to many new situations. A child sniffling in a corner may not be noticed for a long time in a large group of children. Emotional stability was a serious consideration in deciding where to send our fragile, budding personalities. A small child can easily be overwhelmed by the rigors of group participation, and a large group can be positively overpowering. In a small home nursery school, a mother knows not only her own child, but also the children of her friends and neighbors. In the more intimate environment that the home provides, she is aware of each child's problems, whether they involve sibling rivalry or fear of the dark. She can deal with each child in a more personal way than a teacher with fifteen or twenty children. The sad little child is noticed and soothed before his hurt feelings are exaggerated by being left alone too long. For our mothers, this was a one-time opportunity. The children were not faces in an endless chain of students, but were part of a very special miniature community. When a mother chose *The Daddy Book* to read to her class, she knew none of the children would feel isolated or left out because he had no father. When she discussed families, she knew that children without brothers or sisters needed to feel that their pets were important too.

In the "real world" outside the home, some children will be aggressors, some leaders, and some followers. In the home nursery school children are not sheltered completely from such situations, but learn to cope gradually within a small group of familiar peers. Adults are available for support, but can stand not far away in an adjoining room or doorway during free play, while the children develop self-direction in handling many of their own problems. They learn to help each other with puzzles and to decide among themselves who gets the riding toy first. Because the youngsters are not overwhelmed by a large group of children, they are more willing to take some initiative in playing and working with their friends. Thus, each child is building a foundation of social interaction for the future reality of kindergarten. Each mother sees her own child and his peers in this social setting every five or six weeks, and can evaluate his social behavior firsthand. The reality of human behavior is not disguised or suppressed. There will be flare-ups and some hurt feelings. But with parental patience the child will grow to understand his own feelings and the feelings of others.

When we looked at local nursery schools, we found well-meaning teachers, most of whom genuinely enjoyed their jobs. Goodlad, in his nationwide preschool survey found that, like most preschoolers anywhere, children in the surveyed schools enjoyed themselves, but many of the situations were "pedestrian and unimpressive." On the other hand, pointing out the importance of the early years to the overall development of the child, he warns against exposing children to skills for which they are not yet ready, and stresses the need for close parental association with preschool programs. We wanted more for our children than a babysitting service and "mindless fun"; we wanted them to have the fun that comes from pursuing goals and from learning, and we were ready to adapt the learning situation to each child's abilities. Preschoolers are always asking "Why?" or "How come?" They want to discover things. We tried to help them in this process, dealing with every question as only a mother or a close friend can.

Whether nursery schools are regulated strictly or not at all in your area, you cannot be sure of exactly what your child is experiencing, even if you visit the school before registration. The closest you can come to assuring yourself that your preschooler is being treated in a manner that will benefit him socially, emotionally, academically, and physically is to participate in his learning experience with other teachers who know him well and are familiar with his stage of development. You can learn from them, and they from you.

Is Your Child Ready for Home Nursery School?

Every three-year-old is probably ready to join a home nursery school. In such a school, nothing is demanded of a child that he cannot give. In order to help children become ready for school and other social contacts, it is accepted that to some extent each child has immature qualities. In our group, one boy could not speak well; one did not want to leave his mother; one had a very short attention span; one would not communicate with adults; and one was easily overwhelmed by peer-group stimulation. None of these problems caused any major difficulties; in fact, most of them improved by themselves over a period of time. We tried to introduce the children to a healthy, non-threatening group situation in which they were able to cope. They did not merely cope. They thrived!

In a large public nursery school children must put up with materials designed for the "average" child. Since we could design materials to fit the children, the children didn't have to be stretched to fit the materials, or vice versa. If you know your child well enough to present his needs to other mothers, and if you are able to discuss his progress, or lack of it, he will become acclimated to outside social contacts much faster than if he were left to his own devices. We felt there should be some minimum age, however. Chip, the oldest boy in our group, was nine months older than Matthew, the youngest, so their behavior and abilities did not vary too greatly. While some activities in published preschool workbooks were beyond them, they all easily handled the activities in the "Discovery" chapters of this book.

Are You Ready to Be a Teaching Parent?

If you are excited about the home nursery school concept, you are probably ready to begin teaching. But if you are just looking for a nursery school as a babysitting service, a chance to escape from your child, you probably will not enjoy the weeks when you teach the group. If you don't have time to prepare for your sessions, you may find they turn into free-for-all chaos. A certain amount of free time for the youngsters is valuable, but total free play becomes boring. If you honestly feel you cannot handle five or six children at once, or if you are prone to become upset at the slightest provocation, you should think twice. Perhaps it would not be fair to other members of your group if you are truly too impatient to handle a group of children in a constructive manner.

If you are eager to participate in a home nursery school but doubt your ability to teach youngsters necessary skills, we hope this book can allay your doubts and give you the confidence to establish a productive group that will be as beneficial to you as it will to your child. We have researched and will describe some approved teaching methods and learning aids, as well as many ideas from our personal experience. All of these can be easily adapted to your own home nursery school. Also, it is important to remember that what most mothers may lack in formal training, they make up for in "mothering" experience and enthusiasm. Surprisingly, a standard nursery school curriculum isn't available even to those teachers who may be professionally trained. A mother's common sense, along with this well-planned guide, can be the basis for a successful home nursery school program.

In your home nursery school, with conscientious planning, there is no such thing as teacher or student failure. If the child develops healthy positive attitudes, he will be receptive to new school situations. Elementary school will not "turn him off" before he gets started. Even if experts were to develop a model curriculum for nursery school children, the small home group would still have its place. And with the chaos and other problems prevalent in nursery schools today, many mothers find holding nursery school at home is the best thing they can do for their children.

The first year of school is crucial. If your child is to make the most of future education, he must feel secure and happy in his first exposure to a group-learning situation.

2

Organization Made Simple

Young children need safe, warm homes for their new playing and learning experiences. Mothers need assurance that they are bringing their children to a healthy environment and leaving them with congenial, capable mothers. Finding such a situation means carefully selecting mothers to cooperate on your new venture. If you start with a clear idea of your own goals in mind, the organization of your preschool group can be the first step to a rewarding year of educational adventures for you and your little ones.

The First Contact

Any mother with a preschool-age child can organize a home nursery school. Ideally, such a school is centered in a neighborhood where the homes are close together, but finding quality mothers is far more important than finding ones who live nearby. Originally, our participants' homes were within two miles of each other. When Jason's family moved farther away, we were happy to drive the extra few miles because we knew the children loved being with Jason and his mother.

If you have friends or relatives with young children, these are possible, but not necessarily ideal, candidates for the group. If a child with persistent behavioral problems must be asked to drop out, it's easier to deal with a stranger than to offend a friend. Also, two children who are good friends before school starts may exclude others in the group. An ideal home nursery school includes some children that your child would not normally see on a regular basis. "The Kids," as some of our group called themselves, became special friends with a relationship far different from that of casual neighborhood playmates. Making contact with strangers in an effort to organize a home nursery school is not as difficult as it may seem, and may, in the long run, turn out to be the most successful procedure.

One way to find interested mothers is to place an ad in a local newspaper. The ad itself should be concise and direct; details can be given over the phone as each mother calls. Ours read:

MOTHERS OF PRESCHOOLERS—Are you interested in participating in a free home nursery school that will begin next month? If so, please contact Ruth Tucker, 663-3908.

Identifying yourself by name shows that you are acting openly, and it gives the calling mother a more personal initial contact. Briefly outline what you are going to say on paper ahead of time so you won't forget essential information about the home nursery school. You will need each mother's name and phone number for future meeting plans.

Since you want to be sure of each mother's intentions, stress that strict guidelines will be followed in each home to insure that the children are well cared for and well supervised. Then if the mother is not interested, she can merely say so, and there will be no hard feelings. We did not stress these rules when answering calls on our first ad and found that some mothers who originally agreed to join us eventually backed out. They apparently talked about it with their husbands or friends and had second thoughts about going into the school blindly. So we tried again, emphasizing teacher preparation, safety standards, and strict controls. This not only helped to weed out mothers who were looking for a free babysitting service, but it encouraged Jeff's, Jason's, and Chip's mothers to join us. Our emphasis on guidelines helped them overcome their hesitancy about us as potential teachers of their children.

The major drawback in newspaper advertising is the impersonal nature of the contact. A telephone voice doesn't invite as much trust as person-to-person contact. When you talk to the prospective participants, ask them to put off their decisions about joining the group until they have had an opportunity to meet the other mother-teachers and tour their homes.

For a more personal approach, take a walk or ride your bike with your child through your own neighborhood. On a nice day there are always young children outside playing with their mothers close by. Introduce yourself and suggest the nursery school idea to your neighbors. You may gain a friend for yourself and your child even if the mother is not interested in your plan. Such a method may be more time-consuming than placing a newspaper ad, but it may be well worth your effort. Another way to personally contact mothers would be through your church or synagogue, the YMCA, vacation Bible school, your community center, or some other organization where mothers of young children can be found.

Once you have made the initial contacts, set up an organizational meeting at a time convenient for all interested mothers. Schedule the meeting early enough in the day to allow time for a general discussion of home nursery school goals, rules, and size; and follow up with a tour of interested mothers' homes. A second meeting to work out the actual operating details can be held after mothers have discussed the program with their families.

The First Meeting

At your first meeting, be prepared to detail the goals and priorities of the home nursery school and to point out the advantages it has over the traditional nursery school. Stress the cooperative nature of the project by encouraging the interested mothers to add their ideas and suggestions. Next, go over a list of goals and priorities. Reemphasize that this home nursery program is not a babysitting exchange. It involves a well-structured, planned daily routine, developed to excite and interest young children while at the same time aiding in their physical and emotional development.

Priorities and Goals. In our home nursery school we concentrated on several areas of the children's development and formulated goals and priorities that included the following points:

(1) Personal enjoyment is most important for each child. If the child does not enjoy himself, he will not learn well, and he may develop negative attitudes about learning.

(2) The child should learn more about himself. Knowing his name, address, age, and weight helps him discover who he is. Identifying himself as a "good helper," a "big boy," or a "fast runner" helps him realize he has special qualities. The teacher should emphasize the child's positive traits.

(3) Social development of the child helps him succeed in many other areas of his life. This goal involves interaction with other children as well as respect for adult authority. Sharing, showing concern for a sick friend, and taking turns are valuable concepts to learn early.

(4) Awareness of nature's wonders is an important development for a young child, and the teaching mother should emphasize this in all aspects of the home nursery school. Whether it be watching a squirrel bury nuts, looking at the reflection of trees in a lake, or listening to a picture-book story about animals, nature study can be an effective means of helping a child understand his environment.

(5) Physical development of the child helps him perform all his tasks better. Daily exercises are an important part of the schedule, and there are a variety of children's games that provide an enjoyable means of improving a youngster's coordination and strength.

(6) Learning tools such as the alphabet, numbers, shapes, colors, and likenesses and differences are important to children, but they must not be presented in a difficult and tedious manner. If a child finds pleasure in sharpening his skills, he will be anxious to learn more and be better prepared for formal schooling.

Safety Rules. In most cases, there are no laws that regulate the safety and health standards of a small, home-operated, parent-cooperative nursery school. The licensing rules in appendix two will help you decide what is required in your state. Even if you don't need a license, it is essential that strict standards be set up for each home. Most of the criteria should be commonsense rules already in practice in the home. These safety and health rules can be divided into three categories involving home safety, health, and automobile safety.

Home Safety

Fire Prevention. All homes should be equipped with a smoke alarm. Home inspection (often done free by local fire departments) and fire drills can also be very helpful.

Accident Prevention. Each mother should take particular precaution to eliminate poisonous chemicals, dangerous objects, or exposed electrical wiring.

Emergency First Aid. All mothers should have an up-to-date first aid manual close at hand, and emergency phone numbers should be readily accessible.

Strict Supervision. The teaching mother should not leave the children unsupervised even for the length of a short telephone conversation. She should explain to callers that she will return their calls when nursery school is over.

Health Precautions

Home Cleanliness. A clean house is essential, but mothers should be particularly concerned about having a clean bathroom and clean floors wherever children will be playing.

Mid-Morning Snack. Mothers should plan to serve a nonsweet snack, and should avoid serving anything to which the children may be allergic. Throw-away cups should be used for drinks, and paper towels should be available for drying hands.

Emergency Sickness. Each mother should be aware of any allergies that a child may have. If a sudden illness occurs, the child's mother should be contacted immediately, but the phone number of each child's personal physician should be kept handy should it be needed.

Automobile Safety

Travel Rules. Car doors should be locked when children are riding, and each child should be belted in, if possible.

Crossing Streets. If a child is being brought home by another mother, his mother should meet him at the car and help him out. Youngsters should never be allowed to cross the street alone, even if there is no oncoming traffic.

Field Trips. Two adults should be present for field trips. One can concentrate on the driving, while the other takes responsibility for the children.

Other Topics. Another topic to be discussed is the size of the home nursery school. We found that a group of five children worked out very well. If fewer than five mothers attend the organizational meeting, you may want to discuss how to interest other mothers. Enrolling more than six or seven children could cause problems; few homes can accommodate, and few mothers can handle, a larger group for a two-to-three-hour period. If eight or more mothers are present at the meeting, they may decide to split into two groups, according to the location of their homes.

After you talk about goals, rules, and size, some mothers may feel that a home nursery school is not for them. Since others may still be uncertain, a home tour may ease some apprehension. Of course, mothers should know of the tour ahead of time. It should not be considered snooping into someone's private domain; any good mother wants to see where her child will be going to school. When we toured each other's homes, we learned we had several things in common and soon found ourselves admiring each other's kitchen-remodeling jobs. Finding out more about each other reassured us and helped form the basis for a closer relationship. After the tour, the mothers may set a date for their actual planning meeting. Meanwhile, they can discuss the program with their families.

The Second Meeting

All mothers who plan to participate in the nursery school should try to acquire their own copies of this book from a local bookstore or library. This will give them a concept of their responsibilities as well as a picture of the adventures awaiting their youngsters. Now comes the time to discuss such flexible issues as meeting days, time, transportation, and alternating teaching schedules. On these items, each group of mothers must decide what's best for everyone. In our group we originally decided to meet Monday, Wednesday, and Friday mornings from nine o'clock until noon. After several weeks, however, some mothers felt that three hours was too long, and we began dismissing school at 11:30. To maintain continuity in the teaching program, each mother taught the home nursery school for an entire week on a rotating basis. This allowed the teaching mother to develop her daily routine around a particular theme. It also allowed enough time for children to learn new songs and nursery rhymes introduced to them on the first day of the school week. Our solution to the transportation problem was very simple: each mother was responsible for getting her child to school, and the teaching mother returned the children to their homes.

Since a home nursery school is a personalized preschool, organized to meet the needs of its members, no two home nursery schools will be alike. What works in our town may not work in an apartment house. However, although minor organizational details may differ, the teaching sessions will not vary greatly. If one person in the group were to have a large finished room in her basement or elsewhere and wanted to have school at her home all the time with different mothers teaching, the group should seriously contemplate that option. Or if the nursery school revolves around a particular church that has facilities available to the mothers, it would be an opportunity well worth considering. If the group of mothers is large, consider team teaching.

Before winding up the planning meeting, each mother should submit the following vital information regarding her child: name, address, phone number, age, birthdate, parents' names, father's business phone number, name of another person who can be contacted in case of emergency, name and phone number of the child's doctor, and a list of any allergies or health problems of which the teaching mother should be aware. In addition to the personal information, emergency phone numbers such as fire department, police, ambulance, and poison control center should be listed. Assemble the information, and make sure that each mother gets a copy to keep by her phone.

A valuable aid to your fellow teachers at this time would be to inform them of particular personality traits of your child. Mention if your child is hard of hearing or especially aggressive or shy. This will open the way for them to discuss their own children at greater length. It helped us to know that Matthew was shy with all adults and that his initial quietness wasn't due to a lack of appreciation for the teacher. Knowing what the children are like also helps to determine your first teaching rotation. It may work best if mothers teach their first session in pairs, meeting at each home once before settling into your particular group's schedule. This way, the mother of a shy child may either hold the session at her home or accompany her child to his first school session.

To get the children acquainted before the first day of school, you may want to plan an informal get-together in a park. Children may play together while the mothers talk with each other and observe.

Once the school is in full swing, plan to meet periodically to discuss the program and work out unforeseen problems that may have arisen. These meetings can be scheduled following one of the school sessions while the children play close by. At this time you can also discuss the themes you will follow for your teaching weeks.

After meeting the mothers and children in your new nursery school and planning your goals, rules, and schedules, think about what lies ahead. Children are greatly influenced by their teachers, and you are soon to assume a new and important role for your child and his new friends. In addition to being mother, you are soon to be teacher.

3

When Problems Arise

No matter how enthusiastic you are for the home nursery school program, and no matter how much effort you expend in organizing your group and preparing for your own teaching, things may not go as smoothly as you had hoped. Problems are inevitable. A child's first experience in school, and a mother's adjustment to it, often arouses feelings of apprehension. You must be prepared to accept a few unpleasant incidents as part of your teaching experience and as a necessary aspect of your child's development. Remember, success depends on you. Whether a problem is solved, or whether it turns into a crisis, depends largely on how you respond. When problems do arise, seek natural solutions that are suitable for you and your little one.

Perhaps the most common problem faced by any parents of a preschooler is the child's fear of leaving his mother. Children who are otherwise outgoing and friendly may wilt when it comes time for mommy to leave. The separation will not be as difficult in the relaxed atmosphere of a home nursery school as it would be in a strange building with a large group of children, but we found we were by no means immune to the problem. In the first weeks of school Jason cried and clung to his mother, and she gently tried to reason with him. To avoid a traumatic experience, his mother usually ended up staying with him for the first fifteen or twenty minutes of school. Once the activities were in full swing and Jason was busily involved with the other children, she would slip out quietly without him noticing. While this temporarily eased the situation, it did not resolve the basic problem of Jason's fear of separation.

How does a child overcome this fear that plagues so many little ones? Jason's solution came quite by accident. One day Matthew needed a ride to school and Jason's mother offered to pick him up. Matthew hopped into the car with his usual enthusiasm, which soon rubbed off on Jason. By the time they arrived at Chip's house, where school was being held, Jason had forgotten all about his fear of leaving mommy. Both boys jumped out of the car and hurried into the house, almost forgetting to wave good-by. If your child experiences similar fears, it would be well worth your while to offer a ride to an enthusiastic child, even if it means driving out of your way.

Another problem that we as teaching mothers faced was the difficulty of handling our own children in our own homes. In fact, all of the mothers in our group experienced this frustration. Our children became very possessive about their toys, books, and other belongings when nursery school was meeting in their own homes. Though little ones must learn to share, we also thought it was important to respect their feelings about their possessions; forcing the situation often only made things worse. If we set certain toys and games aside to be used only for nursery school, the "home" child expressed much less selfishness. Using books from the local library also helped. Most of the time, you will have to rely on common sense to prevent friction between your child and the others. Don't bring out your child's brand new tricycle with the expectation that he will want to share and the others will calmly line up to take turns.

The problem of sharing was not the only difficulty mothers faced with their own children. Some of the mothers found that their children tried to take advantage of them as teachers. It may be natural for a little one to respond to his friend's mother as a teacher, but with his own mother, it is often a different matter. Let your child know that you expect him to treat you as a teacher during nursery school; prepare him for the session by explaining to him exactly what kind of behavior you expect. We discovered that if we put each of our children "in charge" while school was in his own home, many of the problems were alleviated. The extra responsibilities, such as leading exercises or passing out napkins at snack time, channeled his energy in the right direction. The other children looked forward to being leader when school met at their homes and at the same time they learned to accept the leadership of one of their peers.

As a teacher, you may also face behavioral problems. If you have a normal bunch of preschoolers, you will witness many little tussles accompanied by pushing, shoving, and occasional harsh words. Be positive in your approach; don't turn a minor scuffle into a crisis. Suggest alternatives. One mother ended a struggle between Chip and Matthew over a blue crayon by enthusiastically suggesting to Matthew that a green bird would be just as pretty as a blue one.

If two children want the same toy, encourage them to take turns. Once each child knows what is expected of him, don't be too quick to intervene in minor skirmishes. Children should be watched closely to prevent needless physical confrontations, but they should be given a chance to remind each other to behave. In order to develop self-control, youngsters need the opportunity to work out their own differences. If left alone, children often settle their own disagreements, sometimes through the intervention of another child. The best control of unacceptable behavior is open disapproval by the other children in the group. When children begin monitoring themselves, they develop lasting patterns of healthy group behavior.

If two children do get into a heated quarrel, take charge of the situation. Quickly kneel down and hold the more aggressive one so that his arms are restrained. Look him directly in the eye and speak firmly. This approach has a more immediate calming effect than shouting or grabbing him roughly. If further discipline is necessary, insist that the offenders sit out of the next game or group activity.

Be realistic about children's behavior. Don't be overly anxious about the fact that one child may be aggressive, sometimes taking things from another child who is withdrawn and afraid to assert himself. On the other hand, no one child should dominate the group. If that happens, you have lost control, and the withdrawn child may retreat even further. Try to encourage the quiet youngster to be a leader once in a while. Perhaps he can be the "policeman" and tell the aggressive child where to park his car. Remember, though, that whether a child is withdrawn or aggressive, he won't magically change his behavior just because he is in nursery school. A home nursery school is a preschooler's mini-world, and each child must learn to deal with different types of personalities and situations in his own way. As a teacher, you can guide the behavioral patterns to a certain degree, but each child is a unique individual.

Of course, one child's self-expression cannot be allowed to disrupt a nursery school. A child whose behavior is uncontrollable inflicts an emotional strain on the other children and on a teacher. He is not suited for a home nursery school — or any nursery school, for that matter. If a youngster's attitude and actions continually destroy the harmony of the group and the relaxed atmosphere you are attempting to maintain, there may be only one recourse. Talk to the child's mother frankly in a group meeting. If all the teaching mothers are having the same problem, it may be decided by the group that it would be best for the offending child to discontinue the program. On the other hand, if the other mothers do not see his behavior as a problem, you can learn ways to handle his personality more effectively. Asking a mother to withdraw her child may cause disappointment and hard feelings, but it is the only suitable remedy for severe behavior problems.

Most of the difficulties you will face with preschoolers will be simple to deal with. In fact, many of them will be solved before you begin if you have effectively prepared yourself as a teacher. Though our group was comprised of five lively boys, we had no serious difficulties.

Dealing with the children is the easiest part of developing a home nursery school. Working harmoniously with their mothers is somewhat more complicated. There is always a potential for friction, especially among mothers who are most concerned about the welfare of their children. The home nursery school setup requires each participant to work very closely with the other mothers in the group. Each one plays a vital part in the decision-making process. This has its distinct advantages, as outlined in chapter one, but working closely with other people can pose problems.

Differing ideas and opinions that can cause conflict will arise in any group of people working together. Children who encounter such a situation usually express themselves immediately and openly, and the disagreement is soon settled. Problems among adults may be less easily resolved. Each family raises children according to its own standards, and these individual differences must be respected. In order for a parent co-op group to succeed, all opinions and preferences must be expressed openly and honestly. In addition, mothers must be receptive to the ideas of others.

Come to each of your planning meetings prepared to exchange ideas. Express openly any problems which may have arisen. A simple statement, such as "I'm having trouble getting all the children to pick up the toys," invites comments from the other mothers and helps them feel free to express their own minor troubles. Thus a small annoyance doesn't snowball into a large disagreement.

If one child has a persistent behavioral problem, don't cover it up until it develops into an explosive situation. Ask the child's mother immediately if she has suggestions for coping with the biting or hitting; a mother who is concerned about her child's social development will be anxious to help correct his bad habit. And, of course, be realistic about your own child's behavior. You probably wouldn't be hearing about the same problem from several mothers in the group unless there was something to it.

Each mother should make her idiosyncrasies known to the group. One might object to a child riding in the front seat of a car, another to chewing gum or going barefoot outside. If these sources of annoyance are stated openly, misunderstandings won't surface later on. It is important for members of the group to maintain close contact. If a child bumps his head or gets a bruise or cut while he's in school, the teaching mother should explain the circumstances to the child's mother rather than rely on the child's explanation of what happened.

Many problems can be avoided if the first planning meetings include frank discussions on discipline, behavioral expectations, and child-rearing in general. If the goals and philosophy of the group are precisely formulated and the expectations of each mother and child are clearly spelled out, problems will be kept to a minimum.

Above all, the home nursery school is a businesslike arrangement. While the mothers involved may be friends and neighbors, their planning meetings must not turn into gossip sessions. The task of introducing a little child to his first

39

schooling experience requires efficient planning and problem solving, and meetings should concentrate on the nursery school, the little ones involved, and teaching techniques. *After your meeting there will be plenty of time for friendly conversation.*

A home nursery school requires conscientious dedication on the part of each mother. She must be dependable as a teacher, and she must also fulfill her responsibilities as a mother. However, this does not mean that the school schedule must be rigid. One of the unique advantages of a home nursery school is that it permits flexibility to suit the various members of the group. When one of the families in our group moved, the other mothers were glad to make scheduling changes until the family was settled.

Last-minute scheduling changes and cancellations should be avoided, if at all possible. When an emergency forces cancellation, a substitute should be available. If each mother in the group has one day's activities set aside as a substitute day, the school program can go on without interruption.

In summary, if the mothers in your group freely communicate with one another, are conscientious in their own duties, and above all are considerate of each other's feelings and differences of opinion, your school is bound for success. This does not mean you will have no problems, but you will be able to deal with the difficulties that arise and together seek and find solutions.

4

Effective Home Teaching

To be a successful home nursery school teacher, you must make the best possible use of the resources available to you. You must evaluate your community, your home, and yourself for opportunities. Perhaps any one mother or any particular home can't match the quality of a well-trained, experienced teacher and an established, well-equipped school. But with a little ingenuity, a group of mothers, combining talents and home environments, can provide a broad range of learning experiences and fun for young children that would equal or surpass almost any nursery school.

Evaluate Your Community

Opportunities abound in any community to broaden the scope of nursery school activities. Our community of 15,000 offered many intriguing possibilities. Parks, playgrounds, and museums are the obvious public places for nursery school visits, but there are many more. Recently a museum opened in Washington, D.C., featuring a program specifically designed for very young children. Check your area for such programs. You may have to spend some time reading newspapers, consulting bulletin boards, reviewing brochures, and making phone calls, but it is all part of your new "profession" as a nursery school teacher.

Most public libraries have special programs for young children that can be an exciting supplement to a home nursery school. Our county reference library provides a well-supervised forty-five minute session each week consisting of a story period, films, and puppet shows. Besides adding an interesting sidelight to our nursery school, the program gave the teaching mother a mid-morning break to relax and browse through the library while the children sat open-mouthed in front of the puppet theatre.

In some areas, particularly inner cities, government-sponsored community centers offer programs geared to preschoolers. Pet stores, music stores, florists, bakeries, farms, artists' studios, service stations, factories, and churches can provide interesting field trip opportunities. Relatives and friends who work in such places would probably be willing to provide a short tour. In a music store preschoolers would be fascinated with the shiny trumpets, clanging cymbals, and odd-shaped tubas demonstrated by a friendly store owner.

If you live in or near a large metropolitan area, the field trip possibilities are limitless. Your portable group of five or six children can easily fit into a family station wagon along with two mothers. With our community less than an hour's drive from Chicago, we had easy access to cultural opportunities such as the Shedd Aquarium and the Museum of Science and Industry, which offer programs specially designed for young children. An airport visit can be an exciting field trip for young children. There they can observe not only giant planes, but also loading trucks and taxis and the variety of workers in multi-colored uniforms.

Shopping malls often have free exhibits for their customers. During Fire Prevention Week, we visited our local indoor mall. Volunteer firemen took special care to show the little ones the fire hoses, ladders, and rescue equipment on the shiny fire engines. The boys talked about the trip for months afterwards.

Long-distance field trips, however, should probably be kept to a minimum for three- and four-year-olds, and you should be constantly looking for outing ideas within close walking distance of your homes.

Discovering what is available in your own immediate neighborhood for preschool activities may be a pleasant surprise to you. We found an abundance of places to go for mid-morning walks, all within a few blocks of our five homes. Children enjoyed quacking at the ducks in a duck pond, romping in a large open field, and pressing their noses close to a pet-store aquarium. They swang and twirled in a playground park, explored a large wooded area, and rambled through a fairground, which had a small zoo, a swimming lake, and picnic tables. Observing tractors, cranes, and other earthmoving equipment at construction sites can also be a time of learning and enjoyment for preschoolers. Be sure to have adequate supervision so such outings don't become dangerous.

Take a walk around your own neighborhood, and you'll no doubt discover many things that seem commonplace to you, but that would make interesting visits, especially for children not living in the immediate vicinity. You may want to have a particular theme for each one of your outdoor treks, such as watching birds, picking flowers, or gathering different kinds of nuts and seeds.

With a small group of children, it is easy to arrange for extracurricular activities that do not fall within the prescribed nursery school time period. For example, when one of the mothers in our group heard of a free "Pink Panther" show at a local shopping mall, she made it an extracurricular activity and invited the other children to come along. Another mother learned of a gymnastics program which was being offered at a nominal cost for preschoolers. She informed the other mothers, and soon some of the children were tumbling and jumping together in the same class.

Evaluate Your Home

Searching your community is only the first step in preparing to be a nursery school teacher. Next you must evaluate your own home to see how it can be put to its best use. A large home and yard are desirable, but certainly not essential for an enjoyable learning situation. Of course, the house and yard must be clean and free from trash and debris; a home that can't provide a safe "playground" is not suitable for a nursery school.

Most nursery school activities are well suited to a well-kept, moderate-sized apartment or home. A family room or living room works well for story and song time, as well as for exercises and free-play activities. The kitchen is usually more suited for paper work, crafts, and any other table activities that may have to be followed by a broom or a mop. This will save you the trouble of removing glue from a fine carpet. Variety can be added to your teaching sessions by seating the children on a safe stairway for story time. Creativity is the key to making use of a home's facilities. If it's clean and warm, an unfinished basement is a perfect place for a sandbox during the winter months. An attached double garage is an ideal recreation room on rainy or snowy days.

Purchasing teaching aids and materials is costly, so it is important to make wise use of things you already have. It is also important to set certain things aside to be used only for nursery school activities. In our group a large canister of colored blocks, a giant-sized ABC puzzle, Sesame Street records, and a large Tinkertoy set were used only for nursery school sessions. (Jason's older sister didn't even know that Sesame Street records were in her house until she stayed home with the group on her school's conference day.) Materials can often be purchased cheaply at garage sales. When a local nursery school had a going-out-of-business sale, two of our mothers were first in line for the bargains. Some of our mothers were able to make teaching materials at little or no cost. With a little artistic talent, homemade flash cards and charts can be as attractive as manufactured ones. Flannel graph boards are easy to construct by stapling a piece of flannel cloth to a board backing. Magazine cutouts or your own paper creations backed with sandpaper or felt may be applied to these boards.

Every kitchen and even your wastebasket are good sources of "raw materials" for crafts and paperwork. Start saving things you used to throw away. Here's a partial list of valuable raw materials:

egg cartons
milk cartons
plastic lids, jar lids of all kinds
cardboard from cereal boxes, snack boxes, disposable
    diaper boxes
oatmeal and salt containers
sponges
magazines, calendars, greeting cards
colored paper, wrapping paper, wall paper
stationery boxes

44

"twist 'ems" from bread loaves
paper bags
ribbon, yarn, lace
bottlecaps, corks
margarine tubs, cottage cheese containers, yogurt
  cups
spools
paper-towel and toilet-tissue tubes

Often a whole family may participate in a home nursery school. Story time with one of the dads can give a new perspective to Curious George's adventures. Children watch intently as a father gets his hands black and greasy while changing the oil in the family car. And what a delightful experience for preschoolers to learn an old-fashioned nursery rhyme from grandma, who may be spending a few days with the family. Brothers and sisters, too, enjoy being teacher's helper. Johnny, home from school during teachers' conferences, can bring out his clarinet and demonstrate what a pro he has become after only six weeks of lessons. Family members can help prepare for teaching sessions, also. Asking older children to help cut pictures from magazines will give them a sense of satisfaction and participation.

Evaluate Yourself

It is very important that you make use of your full potential. Some mothers in our group refreshed talents that they had forgotten for years. One mother brought out her guitar that had been collecting dust in the closet. Another, who had previously been embarrassed to play for an audience, entertained the children with her accordion and was heartened to see the bright-eyed children marvel at her talents. A former cheerleader taught the children how to do a simple cheer.

Think back to your own high school or college years. Did you play a musical instrument? Were you involved in gymnastics? Did you have a role in the class play? The areas in which you may be able to excel as a teacher are limitless. Don't be concerned with the abilities of the other mothers in your group — just make the best use of your own. If you feel that you lack

45

creativity and have no artistic, musical, or athletic skill, don't be discouraged. A personal characteristic such as a calm, easygoing temperament or a warm sense of humor can be a strong influence on young children. Don't underestimate yourself. If you make a conscientious effort to succeed, you no doubt will.

Prepare Ahead

"I would not like to count the days when I awoke with a start realizing that it was my turn and I had no projects or ideas. Then there were the many so-called brainstorms I had which I thought would keep my charges occupied all morning but turned out to be disastrous flops." This candid admission was made by a woman who, with several other mothers organized a preschool group, and then wrote of her experiences. "Keeping this age group occupied constructively," she wrote, "is a drain on mind and muscle."* This view of ever-active three- and four-year-olds will find many sympathizers, but providing outlets for their energy is a better answer than throwing up your hands in despair.

It is absolutely essential that each mother involved in the home nursery school prepare for her teaching sessions ahead of time. If you wait until the morning of the day you are in charge, it's only natural that you will experience "disastrous flops." You can educate, excite and entertain preschoolers in many ways, and your morning gatherings need not be a drain on your mind and muscle. The key to success is to be always at least one step ahead of the situation. Many projects calling for advance preparation are available in this book. Prepare several in advance.

It is important to plan your lessons at least a week or two ahead of time in order to make certain that you have the necessary materials and that the storybooks you want are available in the local library. If, for example, you need four milk-bottle caps for each child's craft project, you can request contributions from the other mothers. Librarians are more than willing to suggest stories that will go along with your weekly themes.

*Harriet M. Watts, *How to Start Your Own Preschool Playgroup* (New York: Universe Books, 1973).

(This preparatory visit can be fun for you and your child. Our boys loved going to the library, sitting on the tiny chairs, looking at the fish in the aquarium, and picking out a special book for daddy to read to them at home. It's best, however, to save your nursery school book as a surprise for the actual session, so your child sees it for the first time with the rest of his friends.)

Field trips always should be arranged ahead of time. When one of the mothers in our group realized that it was nearing the time for Twiggy, the family dog, to get her annual shots and check-up, she consulted the local animal clinic and arranged for a field trip. The receptionist and doctor welcomed the children and let them watch Twiggy getting her shots, something they had all experienced themselves. They were delighted when the doctor gave them each a plastic hypodermic syringe (without the needle, of course), which Matthew couldn't wait to take home and try out on his little brother. This field trip required little planning on the part of the mother; the children enjoyed themselves and were able to relate their experience to a book they had read about a pet hospital; and Carlton's dog was immunized in the process. Prior planning for each individual teaching day will be more routine but just as essential as planning for field trips.

Schedule Your Day

For each actual teaching day, it is helpful to set up a schedule such as this:

9:00–9:10	Free play
9:10–9:25	Theme story with discussion
9:25–9:35	Exercises and games
9:35–9:50	Learning skills, songs, and rhymes
9:50–10:00	Chores
10:00–10:10	Paper work
10:10–10:20	Rest period
10:20–10:30	Snack
10:30–10:45	Crafts
10:45–11:05	Outdoor nature hike
11:05–11:15	Music appreciation time
11:15–11:30	Free play

Obviously, no preschool teacher could or even should hold strictly to a rigid schedule, but a written daily program is a valuable aid, especially during your first weeks of teaching. The one above is packed full of activities to accommodate the short attention spans of little ones who have never been to school before. The times and activities can be adjusted when weather prohibits nature hikes and other outdoor doings. If something takes more time than is scheduled, or if the children are especially interested in a certain story, you may wish to save one of your activities for your next session. It is always easier to save an activity for another day than to plan too few and to get caught short.

Sometimes the children will create their own diversions, digressing from a story you are reading to tell about a similar experience they had last summer. One beautiful Indian summer day when the children just weren't responding to any of the structured activities in the program, the teaching mother ignored her schedule and took the youngsters outside on a "treasure hunt" for nuts and pebbles. They enjoyed the warm sunshine one more time before the blustery days of winter arrived.

In the sample schedule, note the alternating of quiet and lively activities. Young children become restless if they are forced to sit still for more than ten or fifteen minutes. It's much better to have them frolic in the yard or kangaroo hop around the room than to have them release their energy by pushing squirmy friends off the sofa. When the kids do get rowdy, as they will at times, you can quiet them by asking them to close their eyes to play a game. Slip off your shoe, and ask them to tell you what it is by touching it. There are many little hints and ideas that can make your daily routine run more smoothly.

Opening Free Play. As you set up your own schedule, seriously consider allowing a short period of free time to begin the day. This gives the children time to become adjusted to one another, and it also fills the time gap between early and late arrivals. When the children are used to the routine, they'll probably ask for a story or craft of their own accord. When it is time to begin the day's activities, each child can take a turn at ringing a little school bell. The leader for the day can round up the others for this ritual.

48

Story Time. After all the children have arrived, story time can begin. A story that centers around the daily or weekly theme should be chosen. Allow the children to react spontaneously, and when the story is finished, discuss how it affects each of them personally. If the theme is pet care, for example, the story should lead right into a discussion on the proper care of their own pets. If a child has no pet, discussion could center on neighborhood pets, a pet he may someday acquire, or his own exotic make-believe pet. The important factor is that the children learn about proper pet care. Have them tug at their own hair. Does that hurt? Do you think it hurts if you pull your dog's hair? Such a discussion makes a lasting impression on the minds of little students.

Exercises and Games. If the group is a lively one, avoid games and exercises that call for excessive bustle. Avoid running games indoors. Instead of throwing hard balls, let children toss a lightweight beach ball. A child's actions are magnified several times when he is with the school group. We found it best to stick with the fairly calm games and exercises explained in chapter fourteen.

Learning Skills, Songs, Rhymes. Learning skills, songs, and nursery rhymes need not be boring or difficult for the children. Reviewing numbers and shapes and learning new concepts can be entertaining if you use your imagination. For example, if you're working on the alphabet, let "Snuffy" your hand puppet have a try. Of course, he'll make mistakes and the children will giggle and snicker as they correct him. When memorizing nursery rhymes and songs becomes tedious, add some finger play. The children will suddenly come alive. Don't be afraid to relax and be a little silly with some of these activities. Hearing the children squeal with laughter will make your day.

Although we scheduled a separate time for learning skills, we found that some of the best opportunities to teach the alphabet, numbers, colors, shapes, and likenesses and differences came during craft or play time. Ask questions like these while the children are playing or working:

"That's a pretty flower. What color is it?"

"What shape is the roof of that house?"

"Can you see any circles in that picture?"

"How many wheels are on that tractor?"

"Does that sandpaper feel rough or smooth?"

"Which animal is bigger in the picture?"

"What sound does the word 'block' start with?"

"How do your lips feel when you say the letter *p?*"

Although the children will not be able to answer every question correctly, they will be learning how to listen, observe, and question for themselves. Matthew hadn't shown much interest in such questions in nursery school, but at home his reaction was entirely different. That afternoon his mother was busy answering questions. "What starts with *b*, Mom? What does 'table' start with? Does 'Mom' start with *m? . . .*" Casual questioning during nursery school activities avoids putting children on the spot, where they may become frustrated and "turned off" if they can't answer.

Chores. Part of becoming an independent person is learning how to perform duties and accept responsibilities. Because children love to imitate adults, our group responded enthusiastically to the idea of a work time. One mother had the children pick peppers from her garden to bring home to their families. Over the course of the year they raked leaves, swept the sidewalk, picked up sticks and papers in the yard, and dusted furniture. Of course, picking up toys after free play is a must.

Paper Work. Paper work should be used not only to help youngsters follow directions, but also to stimulate their thinking processes. If a child is mindlessly coloring, ask him what shape he's making, or what color he likes most. When Carlton appeared to be aimlessly scribbling, the teaching mother asked him what he was drawing. He was quick to respond, "These are roads," as if she should have recognized them right away. Carlton had just returned from a trip to Colorado, where the winding mountain roads had made a lasting impression on his mind. Whether they are coloring in a coloring book or trying to draw "happy faces" freehand, half the fun of paper work for the children is comparing their art work with that of their friends.

Painting is a paper-work activity that youngsters always enjoy. Working side by side at homemade "easels" will help promote a feeling of togetherness. Hang large sheets of shelf or wrapping paper on an old four-by-eight-foot sheet of paneling or plywood. Lean it against a wall, and attach a small sheet of paper for each child so that they can stand next to each other while they paint. For smocks, cut holes for arms and head in old pillowcases, or use dad's old shirts buttoned in back. There are many different types of "paintbrushes": cotton balls, sponge bits, swab sticks, felt, wadded paper towels; or fill shoe-dye bottles with paint and use the daubers as brushes. Often children can have as much fun with "freestyle" fingerpainting or coloring as with structured, preplanned activities. But, as in everything else, too much free activity can lead to disinterest.

Rest Period. Children should have time to take care of their toilet duties before the ten-minute rest period or else the entire time is interrupted by a procession to the bathroom. Encourage the children to be independent in this area. Some three- and four-year-olds still depend on their mothers for assistance in accomplishing their toilet duties, but seeing other children act independently will prompt them to do so too.

While they're resting, the children should lie quietly on a carpeted floor or on throw rugs or mats. We found that using a kitchen timer to clock the ten minutes was the best way to keep the children quiet; they listened intently for the bell to sound.

Snacks. If you use your imagination, snack time will be the most popular period of the day, even if you use only nonsweet snacks, as we did. Cheese can be cut into various shapes with cookie cutters and the children can choose the shapes they want to put on their crackers. They can sprinkle cinnamon on toast, or they can make their own "shish kebab" feasts. They enjoy placing such morsels as seedless grapes, apple wedges, popcorn, wiener chunks, and cheese cubes on the shish kebab sticks (be careful with these!).

A simple task such as popping corn can yield interesting results. While the boys were anxiously watching the corn sizzle in the bottom of the electric popper, Carlton impatiently commanded, "Corn, you better pop!" Then Chip admonished, "If you don't pop, I'll beat you up!" Soon all the boys were joining in bizarre threats to the lagging popcorn. The first popped kernel touched off delighted squeals of laughter.

Crafts. Crafts for preschoolers must be a combined teacher-pupil effort. If the teacher does all the work, the result may be artistic, but the child gets little satisfaction from it. On the other hand, if the child does it all, it is almost impossible, at least in our experience, to make any recognizable objects. Try to establish a happy medium. A child's perception of beauty is much different from an adult's, so every craft should show some of the child's own personality and creativity. If the child is putting an eye where a mouth should be, don't rush in to correct him; he may stop his work and wait for you to do everything for him. There are worse things than having a funny-looking craft. If all the mothers in your group can relax their ideas of beauty, it will be a big help. You won't hover so much over a child if you know his mother doesn't expect ten-year-old work from a three-year-old child.

Nature Hikes. Even if you live in the inner city, outdoor nature walks can be an adventuresome part of the school day. If you have no duck ponds or wooded areas within walking distance, the children can watch birds balance on telephone wires and can squat around busy ants working between cracks in the sidewalks. The best way to keep your charges under tight supervision for such treks is to use a ten-to-twelve-foot rope. Tie knots in the rope about two feet apart, and insist that each child hold onto a knot. This will avoid bunching.

Listening and Participating. When they return from their outdoor hike, the children can relax and listen to records or tell stories. Storybook records, where the book is accompanied by recorded reading and sound effects, are popular among youngsters. *Pete's Dragon* becomes more exciting if the children can hear the creature's grunts in the background. Sometimes children like to tell stories from their imagination, making them up as they go along and perhaps acting them out. Often the children will ask the teaching mother to read a favorite story so they can relax and listen.

Closing Free Play. After a full morning session, the children will be ready to get out the toys for their final free-play period.

This should not be free-for-all time. Educational toys or those that develop small muscle coordination are beneficial. Building sets, beads to string, lacing cards, and puzzles encourage cooperation. Playing with cars invites the children to use their imaginations in many ways; imaginary trips to the grocery store are often interrupted by sirens, fire trucks, and races to the hospital. Dolls can give children a chance to play the roles of mother, father, and even babysitter.

Free play should be a time when the concept of sharing is allowed to bloom. One of our mothers chose to use Tinkertoys for free play, and found it necessary in the beginning to make five very separate and evenly distributed piles for the children. As time went on, however, she found that she could make one large pile in the center of the room, and the children all worked around it. Soon Jason and Chip began building projects together, with Matthew always ready to add the finishing touches.

During free play it is best for the teaching mother to step out of the picture—to be where she can quietly observe the children unnoticed. Children will communicate more freely without the immediate presence of an adult. We found that Jeff, who was otherwise hesitant to join in the conversation, opened up when he was "alone" with his friends. On one occasion, as the children were busily constructing with Tinkertoys, Carlton, as was typical, began relating one of his "tall tales" based on a neighborhood incident. In this one almost everyone he knew was being taken by ambulance to the "hossible."

"It's hospital," Chip immediately advised him.

"Hossible," repeated Carlton, hesitatingly trying to correct himself.

"Hospital," all the children chimed in loudly, and soon Carlton himself was pronouncing it correctly.

Your first weeks of teaching will be the most difficult. It will take time for the new students and new teachers to get settled into the routine and to become adjusted to new materials. At first, the children will probably have little in common, and most of the nursery rhymes and songs you teach them will be new. Later, they'll enjoy reviewing "Itsy Bitsy Spider" when you have a gap to fill in your session. If you become discouraged by the short attention span of your charges, take heart. The children will soon learn to cooperate with each other and to help each other and you through problem situations. Changes in behavior may seem dramatic to you after you haven't taught the children for five or six weeks. This is part of the fun of your new job. Matthew at first hardly spoke a word to any of the teachers, but by the second round he was happily joining in the activities.

Youngsters are just as curious and receptive in a group as they are by themselves. If they are provided with ideas and materials, they ask plenty of questions and are eager to develop skills. Children learn something from almost any activity, even if it is not apparent to an adult, and even if the activity does not go exactly as the teaching mother planned.

Once you are ready to begin your adventure as a home nursery school teacher, review part two of this book to get an overall picture of the ideas offered in the Discovery chapters, which provide enough material for a full year of school, three days a week. Talk with the other mothers about the curriculum and plan ahead for themes you intend to cover in your sessions.

For each week of sessions, choose one or two crafts, several paperwork ideas, and some poems and songs to teach the children. Gather materials for your projects and be sure you can complete them successfully. Visit the library and check out some books and some nursery rhyme records. Select some appropriate exercises that you feel confident about teaching; try them out on your own child so he can help teach the other children. If you choose a recipe for a treat or art project from appendix one, prepare as much as you can in advance to minimize confusion. It's always best to try a recipe out ahead of time so that you will be confident in using it.

The more you do before the children arrive, the more relaxed you will be during the session. Don't feel that you must follow the outlined curriculum precisely. Use your imagination and add your own personal touches. Put a funny-looking hat on Humpty Dumpty, or add some new actions to a nursery rhyme. This will give your teaching sessions the stamp of your own personality.

Part Two

Challenging the Child

5

Discovering Ourselves

When a child learns about himself, he studies a very interesting subject. Emotions of fear, anger, disappointment, love, and happiness dominate his life. Getting in touch with his own feelings and learning to deal with them helps him become more in tune with himself. The three-year-old is past the stage of being diapered and fed and is learning to take care of his own body. He learns what foods are good for him to eat and which ones are bad for his teeth. He discovers how to dress himself and begins to take pride in grooming, willingly brushing his hair and washing his face and hands. He studies his feet after a hot bath and giggles at their puffy wrinkles. He is curious about how his body works, and experiments with his growing muscular coordination. Knowing more about himself emotionally and physically helps him in the important process of growing up.

Paper Work

My Favorite Meal. Cut out food pictures from can and box labels, and let the children choose their favorite foods and paste them on a paper plate. Talk about kinds of foods that make children big and strong, such as meats, vegetables, and fruits.

Building a House. Cut construction paper into squares, rectangles, and triangles of various sizes representing windows, doors, and chimneys. Let the children build their own houses by choosing pieces and pasting them on construction or typing paper. Talk about their own homes and different kinds of houses: two-story, ranch, apartments, cabins, house boats, dog houses, and doll houses.

Traffic Safety Rules. Divide a sheet of paper into three sections. In the first section draw a rectangle containing three circles arranged one above the other, as in a traffic light. Cut red, green, and yellow circles from construction paper to match the circles you have drawn. In the next section draw a smaller rectangle containing two little rectangles, one above the other. Cut rectangles of the same size from red and green construction paper and letter on the red DON'T WALK and on the green WALK. In the last section draw an octagon. Cut a red shape to match, and letter STOP on it. As the children paste the pieces of construction paper in the appropriate places, discuss traffic safety with them.

Finger and Hand Printing. Using a fingerpaint recipe (see Appendix One), make up your own paint and put it in a low round cake pan. Let the children put their hands in and make imprints on paper. They can also make imprints with their fingers, knuckles, and fists. They should wipe their hands on a paper towel or throw-away rag after each print. On a second sheet of paper let them trace their hands with a pencil, leaving enough room for them to trace another family member's hand for comparison. Talk about physical differences in people and how each finger- and handprint is different.

Personalized Crown. Using construction paper, cut crown shapes that will fit the children's heads. Decorate the crowns with small bright colored shapes of paper from Christmas cards or with packaged glue-on stars. Write the names of each child on a crown, or cut out letters and let each child paste his name on. Talk about how each person is special and let the children model their crowns for each other.

Grooming Poster. On a sheet of typing paper let each child trace combs, toothbrushes, soap, and hairbrushes. Use an appropriate caption such as "Things That Make Me Pretty." Discuss the importance of grooming and cleanliness with the children.

Name Puzzles. Trace the letters of each child's name on a cardboard rectangle. Color each letter a different color. Cut the cardboard into an eight or ten piece jigsaw puzzle. Each child will enjoy seeing his name appear as he fits the pieces together.

Identification Doors. This project is done largely by the teaching mother, but the youngsters will have fun with it. Two sheets of construction paper are needed for each child. Cut out three sides of small rectangles, squares, and other shapes from one sheet. Then fold them back so that they will open and shut as doors. On each door, letter an unanswered identifying feature of the child, such as "My name is," "My birthday is," "My address is," and "My phone number is." Glue these sheets to the backing sheets and write the appropriate answer behind each door. Let the children decorate the top sheets by coloring or pasting on paper designs and shapes. Though they cannot read, the youngsters will soon memorize the identifying information and will enjoy opening the doors for the answers.

Silhouettes. Hang a large sheet of paper on the wall. Project the child's shadow profile on the paper. Trace the outline of the profile with a felt marker. Let the child make his own profile facial features with a crayon. Talk about profiles and show pictures of people from the front, side, and back.

Crafts

Vegetable-Can Stilts

Materials: empty vegetable or fruit cans with labels
    colored paper
    five-foot lengths of clothesline

Ahead of time: Collect two cans for each child. Punch two holes near the closed ends. Cut paper circles to cover the ends of the cans. Print the child's first name on one circle and his last name on the other one. Then cut strips of paper 1" wide to fit around each can. On one, letter VEGETABLES HELP. . . and on the other. . . ME GROW BIGGER. If necessary, file sharp edges off the cans.

Kids Do: Help the children to glue name circles on top of the cans and to glue the strips of paper around each can. Then they can push the clothesline through the holes and stand on the cans. Adjust the rope lengths so that each child can walk by pulling the can up against each foot as he lifts it. Talk about fruits and vegetables and about how eating the right foods helps the children to grow and to stay healthy. Let them walk around on their stilts so they can see how it feels to be "taller."

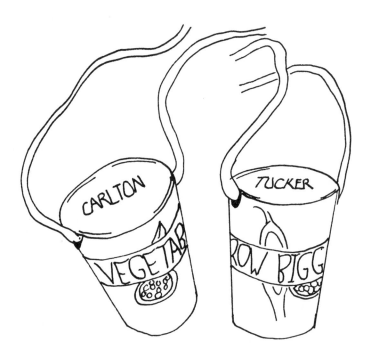

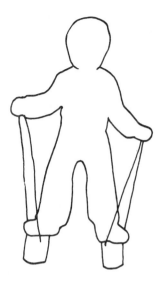

Life-Sized Cardboard Person

Materials: large cardboard paper-towel cartons (panels must
    be larger than a child)
    marking pens
    paints
    "clothes" brought by each child

Ahead of time: With a razorblade cutter, cut out large panels
    from cardboard boxes.

Kids Do: *First Session.* In turn, each child lies flat on a cardboard panel while the teaching mother supervises the other
children in tracing around his body with marking pens. When
they're finished each child can compare his silhouette with
those of the others. *Between Sessions.* Mom cuts out the silhouettes with a razorblade cutter. *Second Session.* Mom draws
facial features and clothing lines according to the children's
instructions. Then they paint their own dolls, guided by mom's
suggestions. Concentrate on the face, because painting the
clothing may take too much time. Sponges may be used to
paint the larger areas. Let the paint dry between sessions.
Third Session. Kids bring old articles of clothing to dress their
dolls.

Fresh Face

Materials: oranges
    whole cloves
    round toothpicks

Kids Do: Each child shows where he would draw eyes, nose, and mouth on his orange. The teaching mother pokes holes with a toothpick where the children have indicated and sticks cloves in the holes and on top of the orange for hair. Each child can place his orange in his bedroom, or wrap it in nylon netting and hang it from a hanger. It will add a nice smell to his room. Ask children if they notice when things smell good and when they smell bad. Do they like the smell of cloves? What are their favorite smells?

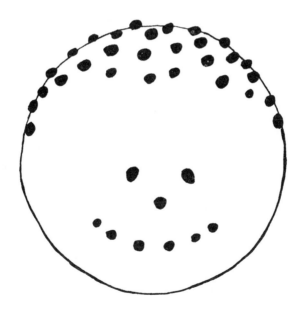

Wig

Materials: lunch bags
    blunt scissors

Ahead of time: Cut a section out of the front panel of each sack
    for the face.

Kids Do: The children cut strips in the bags for hair; some can
be curled with scissors or a pencil. Kids can play with their
new hair and pretend to be different people. Even with similar
wigs do they all look alike? They'll still see differences in eyes,
mouth, and body build.

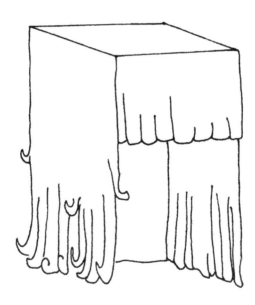

Personal Jewelry

Materials: long cardboard tubes
     rings cut from plastic bottles
     spools
     yarn
     colored paper strips
     old photos of children in your group (optional)

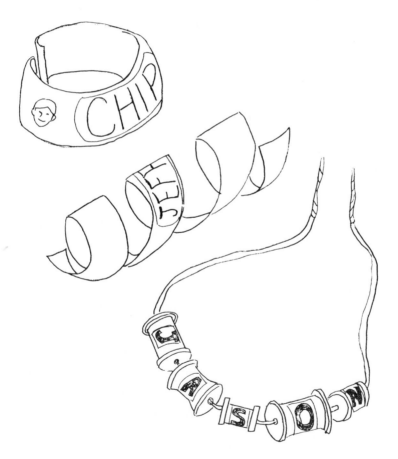

Ahead of time: Cut bands from plastic bottles, and sand the edges lightly. Larger ones can be used as head bands, smaller ones as bracelets. Cut cardboard tubes along seams, and cut the curved strips in half lengthwise for two bracelets. Cut yarn pieces long enough to make necklaces and wrap tape around the ends. For bracelets, write each child's name on a strip of paper. For necklaces, write each letter of the names on a square of paper small enough to fit on a spool as shown.

Kids Do: Each child selects his name to paste on his bracelet, along with a small picture of himself, if he has one. For the necklace, he pastes the letters on individual spools and arranges them in the correct order to spell his name. Then he strings the spools on the yarn to make a necklace.

Talking Face

Materials: heavy cardboard
    paper-towel tubes
    facial features from construction paper
    strips of paper for hair

Ahead of time: Cut out ten-inch ovals for the faces from heavy cardboard. Cut strips of paper for hair, and white one inch circles and colored half-inch circles for eyes. Cut mouth-shaped holes in the faces, just large enough to insert the paper-towel tubes.

Kids Do: Each child pastes the eyes and hair on the face. Mom may help curl the hair with a pencil or scissors, if desired. Mom can help tape the tube to the mouth opening behind the face. The children can talk through the tube when you ask them to say their names, addresses, and phone numbers. Talking behind a mask makes it easier and more fun to join in such activities.

Picture Magnet

Materials: baby food jar lids
     ribbon or lace
     snapshot of each child
     small magnets

Ahead of time: Cut lace or ribbon into pieces seven inches long. Trace around a lid on each child's photo and cut out the circle to fit inside the lid.

Kids Do: Each child puts a small amount of glue on the back of his picture, and secures it inside the lid. After a small ring of glue is put around each picture, the children apply ribbon or lace as frames. Each child can take his picture home and display it on the refrigerator with a magnet.

This is a good time to talk about pictures. What do the children do when their pictures are taken? Do they pose? Smile? What happens when flash bulbs go off? If they seem responsive, have them practice sitting still and posing for a "portrait."

Activities

Discovering the Senses. Using ten baby food jars, fill two jars approximately one-fourth full of rice. Repeat this with raisins, peanuts, tiny pieces of paper, and nuts and bolts. Cover all the jars completely with aluminum foil. Then have the children shake the jars and match those that sound alike.

The sense of taste is fun to experiment with. Blindfold the children one at a time and let each one sample and identify two or three foods. Apple slices, orange sections, pickles, carrot sticks, cheese, and ice cream all work well for this experiment.

The sense of touch can be easily tested. Have each child face away from the group and reach behind his back to feel various objects and identify them by touch alone. Items such as

68

sponges, silverware, crayons, small toys, bananas, apples, and raisins are all suitable for this experiment.

Dressing Ourselves. There are many ways that young children can practice dressing. If you have old shirts that did not sell in last summer's garage sale, cut away all but the button and buttonhole strips and let the children use them to practice buttoning and unbuttoning. The same can be done with old items of clothing that have zippers. Let the children practice putting on their own coats by placing the garment on a sofa with the collar or hood closest to the child. With the coat in that position, the child puts his arms in the arm holes and brings the coat over his head.

Getting Lost. This is a "pretend" game. Each child takes a turn pretending he is lost in a shopping mall or department store. The teaching mother plays the role of a clerk and asks the child to identify himself. She asks appropriate questions and assures him that his parents are searching for him. This game works well for a team teaching project, with one mother playing the part of the clerk and the other the part of the concerned parent. The children have fun playing their parts in the drama, and it also impresses upon them the importance of properly identifying themselves in such situations and reassures them that their parents would be anxiously looking for them.

A Close Look at Hair and Skin. Take a strand of hair from each child and tape it to a sheet of paper labeled with his name. Then let each child have a close look at the hairs through a magnifying glass or microscope to see how they differ. Looking at the palms of their hands and perhaps a sore, cut, or scab that one of the children has will also be of interest to them. Discuss with them how skin and hair are replaced when they are lost.

Clay Hand Forms. Let the children help you mix up a batch of baker's clay (see Appendix One). Divide the clay in equal parts and let the youngsters have fun making impressions with a variety of different household items, such as a table fork, a key, a fingernail file, a wood screw, a thimble, a plastic hair roller, and a cheese grater. After they have experimented with various forms, ask each child to make his clay into a ball and then flatten it out large enough for a hand print. After the hand prints are made (they should be at least one-fourth of an inch deep), make a small hole at the top of each plaque. Follow the recipe directions for baking, and after the plaques cool, let the children paint and decorate them. String bright colored yarn through the holes for hanging.

Field Trips. If you have contacts with anyone who works in or owns a bakery, beauty or barber shop, or children's health clinic, try to arrange for a short tour for the children. When your own little boy is due for a haircut, call ahead and ask if the other children can come along and observe.

Another simple and short field trip idea is to walk with the children to the closest school crossing and chat for a few minutes with the crossing guard about street-safety rules. It will be a good experience for the children to cross the street with the assistance of the crossing guard.

Songs, Rhymes, and Fingerplay

Deedle Deedle Dumpling

Deedle Deedle Dumpling, my son John,
Went to bed with his stockings on;
One shoe off and one shoe on;
Deedle Deedle Dumpling, my son John.

I Saw You in the Ocean

I saw you in the ocean;
I saw you in the sea;
I saw you in the bathtub;
Oops! Pardon me.

There Was a Little Girl

There was a little girl, who had a little curl,
Right in the middle of her forehead;
When she was good, she was very good,
But when she was bad she was horrid.

Little Boy Blue

Little Boy Blue, come blow your horn!
The sheep are in the meadow, the cows are in the corn.
Where is the little boy that tends to the sheep?
Under the haystack, fast asleep!

Two Little Eyes

Two little eyes to look around,
Two little ears to hear each sound;
One little nose to smell what's sweet,
One little mouth that likes to eat.

Teddy Bear, Teddy Bear

Teddy Bear, Teddy Bear, turn around;
Teddy Bear, Teddy Bear, touch the ground.
Teddy Bear, Teddy Bear, shine your shoe;
Teddy Bear, Teddy Bear, I love you.
Teddy Bear, Teddy Bear, go upstairs;
Teddy Bear, Teddy Bear, say your prayers.
Teddy Bear, Teddy Bear, turn off the light;
Teddy Bear, Teddy Bear, say Goodnight.

Ring the Bell

Ring the bell!   [Pull lock of hair.]
Knock at the door!   [Tap forehead.]
Draw the latch!   [Pull up nose.]
Open it up!   [Open mouth.]
And walk in!   [Put finger in mouth.]

Head and Shoulders

Head and shoulders, knees and toes,

knees and toes, knees and toes; head and shoulders

knees and toes, we all turn round together.

This is an exercise song. Children should touch each body part as they sing.

The Mulberry Bush

1. Here we go round the mulberry bush, the

mulberry bush, the mulberry bush;

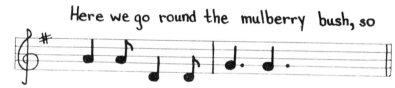

Here we go round the mulberry bush, so

early in the morning.

2. This is the way we wash our clothes ....
   so early in the morning.

3. This is the way we sweep the floor ...
   so early in the morning.

On Top of Spaghetti

Tune: On Top of Old Smokey

On top of spa-ghet-ti all covered with

cheese; I lost my poor meatball when

somebody sneezed.

It rolled off the table and onto the floor,
And then my poor meatball rolled out of the door.

If you eat spaghetti, all covered with cheese;
Hold onto your meatball, and don't ever sneeze.

Storybook Ideas

Let's Find Out About Safety, Martha and Charles Shapp (Franklin Watts, 1964).

The Shy Little Girl, Phyllis Krasilovsky (Houghton Mifflin, 1970).

I Was So Mad! Norma Simon (Whitman, 1974).

Hold My Hand, Charlotte Zolotow (Harper and Row, 1972).

If I Had My Way, Norma Klein (Pantheon, 1974).

The Temper Tantrum Book, Edna M. Preston (Viking, 1969).

Do You Know What I'll Do? Charlotte Zolotow (Harper and Row, 1958).

I Know What I Like, Norma Simon (Whitman, 1971).

Girls Can Be Anything, Norma Klein (Dutton, 1973).

You Go Away, Dorothy Corey (Whitman, 1976).

Noisy Nancy Norris, Lou Ann Gaeddert (Doubleday, 1965).

What Do I Say? Norma Simon (Whitman, 1967).

Taste, Touch, and Smell, Irving and Ruth Adler (John Day, 1966).

Food Is for Eating, Illa Podendorf (Childrens Press, 1970).

6

Discovering Others

Preschoolers know that they're not alone in the world. But they don't quite know how to deal with the various shapes, sizes, and types of people they see. They love to play with little people like themselves, but sharing a favorite toy with a schoolmate isn't always easy. The more children play, the more they realize that working together on a "skyscraper" produces better results than competing for the blocks. They begin to see that there is something to be gained in giving to a friend. The lessons children learn from friends help them as they grow and meet new people.

The first adults children know are their own relatives or the parents of friends. As they realize that different moms and dads have different jobs, they learn more about occupations. As they play "store" in nursery school, they come to understand that store clerks are more than just big people. They, too, can offer help and friendship. As children are exposed to customs of different cultures and ethnic groups, they begin to appreciate the variety of people around them. Nursery school is a miniature society. What children learn there about others helps them when their world expands.

Paper Work

Dressing Up Grandma. Draw a simple form of a woman on a piece of lightweight cardboard for each child. Let the child paste on clothing from an assortment of small skirt and blouse shaped pieces of fabric, adding ribbons, lace, and rick-rack for frills. Use oval pieces of felt for shoes and cottonballs for hair. Talk with the children about grandmas and how special they are. Even if they do not have grandmas of their own, they may know of a special elderly lady who is like a grandma to them.

My Friends' Feet. On sheets of construction paper, have the children trace around each other's shoes with a magic marker. Write the name of each child in his footprints. Encourage the children to talk about their friends and how much fun it is to walk places with them.

Working People. Using magazines or catalogs, cut out pictures of people who represent different occupations. Ask the children to identify the different occupations and to see if they can find those of their moms and dads. Let each child choose some pictures to paste on a sheet of paper, and have him draw a circle around the one that represents the occupation he would like to pursue when he grows up.

Card Puzzle. Give each child an old greeting card that depicts a family or a similar group of people together. Let each cut his card into several pieces with scissors, and then have him put his puzzle together.

"Pretend" Family Book. Preschoolers enjoy making up their own books of pictures. From catalogs and magazines cut out pictures of people of all ages, pets, houses of all sizes, household appliances, tools, and toys. Have each child select a picture of a house to paste on the first page, with a title such as "Chip's Pretend Family." Ask each child to fill the remaining pages by selecting the people and pets that he wants in his family, and let him pick a toy or tool for each family member. Mom might get a typewriter, Dad a lawnmower, and baby sister a stuffed bunny. Encourage the children to make up stories about the characters they have selected, and to "read" their books to their families when they go home.

Indian Headdress. Cut one-inch bands of construction paper, long enough to encircle the top of a child's head. Make feather shapes from construction paper of various colors and let the children glue them onto the bands. Talk about Indians and their special native costumes and dance, and then encourage the children to form a circle and imitate an Indian dance.

77

Walking Postman. On heavy paper draw simple figures of uni-formed postmen with only stumps for legs. Cut the figures out and cut holes large enough for a child's forefinger and middle finger near the end of the stump legs. Have the children color their figures blue. They will enjoy "delivering the mail" by using two fingers to make their postmen walk.

Crazy-Shaped People. Cut out several half-dollar-sized circles of different colors for faces, enough so that there are three or four for each child. Cut out the same number of small triangles and twice the number of small rectangles. The children can paste the circles on a sheet of paper for heads. For shoulders and waist, have the children paste a triangle below the circle, with one point downward. Paste the rectangles under the triangle for legs. The youngsters can complete the faces, hair, arms, and feet with crayons. Talk about how everyone is dif-ferent in some way, and that this is what makes the world interesting.

Family Portrait. Ask each child's mother for a family snap-shot. Cut a circle in a small paper plate large enough to ade-quately frame the photo. Use an uncut paper plate of equal size for backing. Let the children color, paint, or paste cut-out de-signs on the frame, and then help them glue their photos and frames to the backing. String yarn through the top for hanging.

Crafts

Finger-Puppet "Workers"

Materials: cardboard rolls
  colored heavy paper

Ahead of time: Trace hats and collar onto paper, and cut them
  out. Add your own variations. Cut out small circles for
  eyes and tiny ones for buttons; cut mouth shapes; and cut
  two finger-sized holes about half an inch from the bottom
  and half an inch apart in each tube.

Kids Do: Each child pastes features, collars, and hats in their proper places and adds some features with pencil or crayon. Children can play with their finger puppets, pretending to be police officers, nurses, and cowpokes. Talk about different hats people wear, and what jobs they do.

COLLAR

HATS

Baby Cradle

Materials: oatmeal boxes
    ribbon, lace, yarn, doilies
    construction paper or wrapping paper for decorations

Ahead of time: Cut boxes as shown. Cut the end panels from unused halves to make "rockers." Cut paper to match the rockers. Letter BABY on the papers.

Kids Do: Each child pastes decorations or strips of paper on the cradle. Decorate the lid also, pasting a doily on the round part and trimming the edge with lace or yarn. Paste paper half circles onto the rockers as shown. Small dolls, little animals, paper dolls, or clothespin dolls can fit in the cradles.

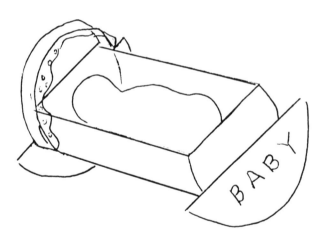

80

Waterproof Canoe

Materials: heavy note paper
     paraffin
     marking pens

Ahead of time: Draw a canoe on note paper as shown. Prepare
     to heat paraffin. Cut out a canoe for each child.

Kids Do: Each child decorates the canoe with markers and
folds it into the proper position to be stapled. Heat the paraffin
to a liquid state. Carefully drop the canoes into the paraffin
and leave them in for one minute. The children dangle ends of

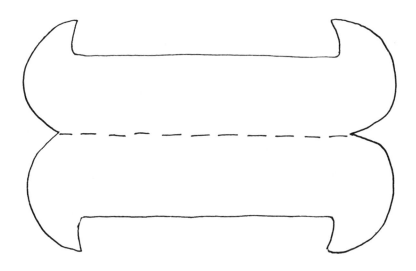

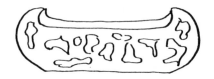

strings in the paraffin while the teaching mother supervises. Later, these strings can be used for bead stringing, because the ends will be stiff.

Try to sail the waxed canoe, and then try to sail a plain piece of paper. Ask the children why the paper behaves differently. Ask them to feel the difference between the treated and untreated surfaces. Would the children like to ride in a canoe? What other kinds of boats have they seen? A book about Indians would be helpful here.

Indian Tepee

Materials: construction paper, heavy wrapping paper of various colors
   blunt scissors
   soda straws

Ahead of time: Cut half circles of construction paper as shown. Ten-inch diameters make nice-sized tepees.

Kids Do: Each child shreads or cuts some colored paper into small pieces and glues them onto half circles in random designs. When the glue dries, roll the tepees into their cone shape, staple them, and cut the tops as shown (2). The tepees may be slit as shown (3), and the door flaps folded back. Each child can turn his tepee on its side and poke straws up through the top of the cone as support poles. Tape the straws to the inside of the tepees.

Talk about what it must be like to live in a tepee. Where would you sleep? How would you cook? What furniture would you have? Would you have your own bedroom? Set up a "tent" by spreading a sheet or blanket over some chairs.

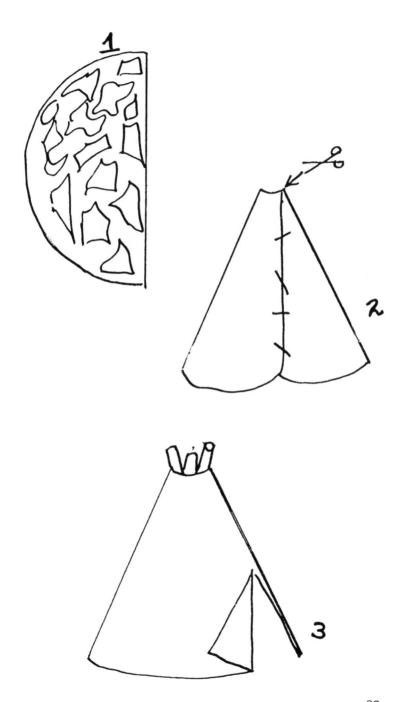

Firefighter's Costume

Materials: small paper bags
   large grocery bags
   red and black paint

Ahead of time: Cut the small bags for the hats as shown. From
   leftover pieces of the bags, cut curved pieces for hat brims.
   Cut a slit up the front side of the grocery bags leading to a
   neck hole at the top.

Kids Do: Each child tries on the grocery bag "coat" while
holes are cut for the arms. He then paints the coat black, the
hat and brim red, and glues the brim to the hat. A white paper
badge can be pasted on the brim. Ask children why firefighters
wear hats and raincoats. Let them wear their costumes and
pretend to be firefighters. Give them a vacuum-cleaner hose to
aim at their pretend fires.

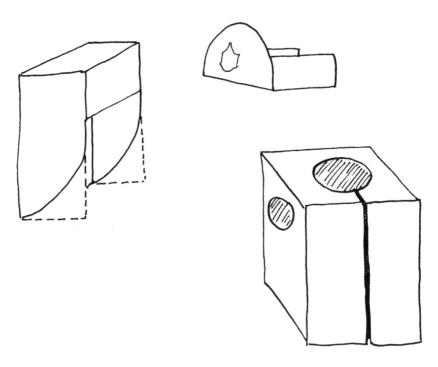

Matchbook Clown

Materials: *empty* matchbooks
    small circus-design seals, designs, or pieces of colorful wrapping paper
    colored paper

Ahead of time: Cut a strip of heavy colored paper, eight inches long and one-half inch wide, and draw and cut out a clown's head about one inch round for each child.

Kids Do: Each child glues colorful designs or wrapping paper on his matchbook. Fold the strip of paper to make a spring, as shown. Glue the bottom to the inside of the matchbook, and the top to the back of the clown's head. Show the children how to close the book, and tell them to surprise their families by making the clown pop out at them. Ask the children if they've ever seen clowns in circuses or toy stores. Are clowns funny? What do they do? Are there real people under all that make-up?

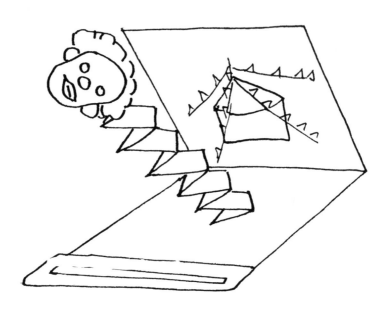

Papier-Mâché Giraffe

Materials: one plastic gallon milk container
    five long cardboard wrapping-paper tubes
    yogurt cup or paper cup
    "twist 'ems"
    yarn for tail
    picture of a giraffe

Ahead of time: Assemble all the materials. Cut holes for legs
    and neck in the milk container. Prepare papier-mâché (see
    Appendix One). Cut a slit in the yogurt cup as shown.

Kids Do: The children can poke legs and neck into the holes.
While the legs are being tied to the body with string, let the
children look at the picture of a giraffe. Ask them where to
place the twist'ems for the ears and horns, and where to put
the head. Wire the twist'ems through the slit in the yogurt cup
and wire the head to the neck. Then let the children cover the
giraffe with papier-mâché. This may take more than one ses-

slit

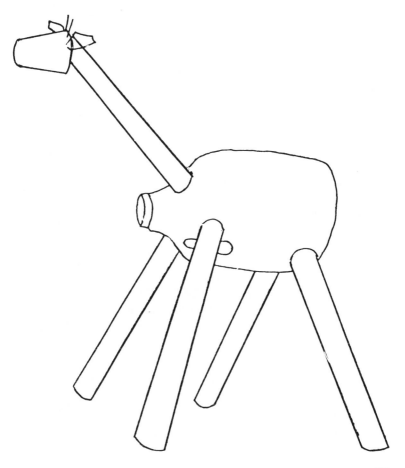

sion. Later, they can paint it, stick on the yarn tail, and glue on buttons for eyes.

This is a cooperative project which should be undertaken only after the children are well-known to each other and the teaching mother. The recipient should be decided in advance and should be someone whom they all know and wish to please, perhaps one of the group who is home sick. While the kids are working on their project, compliment them on how well they work together. Point out that no one of them could have done the project on his own.

Activities

Surprise Treat for the Family. Bake a batch of cupcakes or cookies, and let the children decorate them with frosting and candies. They will enjoy taking them home to their families. Discuss the fun of giving surprise treats to people you love.

Wild West Cowhand. Fit a piece of wire that is three or four feet long inside an eight-foot piece of clothesline. Make a loop with the wire and fasten it together, leaving the five foot tail dangling. This will be your little cowhands' lasso. Gather all your stuffed animals, and let each child see how many wild creatures he can rope. Talk about cowhands and how they differ from farmers and other people who work with animals.

Buying and Selling. Save empty cereal, cake mix, and other food boxes, as well as cans (open them from the bottom and leave the label intact). Let the children play store with paper money. Make sure each child has a turn to be storekeeper. Have a supply of empty bags so that each child can carry away his favorite foods.

Caring for Baby. If there is a baby in your home, it is an ideal opportunity for children to see how babies are cared for. Since this is commonplace for your own child, let him be the helper in this activity by having him assist you in changing the diaper, rubbing on some vaseline or powder, or even giving baby a bath. The other children will want to join in dressing baby.

Point out how tiny the baby's toes and fingers are, and how helpless the baby is compared to the preschoolers. Obviously, the youngsters must be well supervised for this, and it would be well not to involve a tiny infant.

Dressing Up. Present the children with a wide assortment of old clothes, shoes, belts, jewelry, hats, purses, gloves, and stockings and let them choose what to wear and whom they wish to represent. Encourage them to act out the role of the person or occupation they are representing.

Using the Telephone. When one of the children in your group is home with a cold, call the child's mother and ask if the other children could talk to him for a few moments on the phone. Encourage the children to identify themselves, to assure the sick child that he is missed, to tell about their activities of the day, and to wish their classmate well.

Field Trips. Visiting the firehouse or police station is always interesting for young children and ties in closely with the theme of appreciating others and their occupations. Be sure to call ahead to arrange for a tour.

If there is a rest home for the elderly nearby and if the director feels a visit from the children would be appropriate, a short program of songs at holiday-time could bring joy to both the residents and the children. Or perhaps relatives or neighbors who are shut-ins might welcome a visit from the nursery school.

Songs, Rhymes, and Fingerplay

My Family

This is my father;	[Point to thumb.]
This is my mother;	[Point to index finger.]
This is my brother tall.	[Point to middle finger.]
This is my sister;	[Point to ring finger.]
This is the baby;	[Point to little finger.]
Oh, how I love them all.	[Clap hands.]

Bye, Bye Baby Bunting

Bye, bye, baby bunting,
Daddy's gone a hunting,
To get a little rabbit skin,
To wrap the baby bunting in.

Old Woman Who Lived in a Shoe

There was an old woman who lived in a shoe;
She had so many children, she didn't know what to do.
She gave them some soup and whole wheat bread;
They picked up their toys and went straight to bed.

Grandma's Glasses

These are Grandma's
    glasses;   [Make circles with thumbs
                               and index fingers around eyes.]

And this is Grandma's hat.   [Cup hands on top of head.]
This is the way she folds
    her hands,   [Fold hands.]
And lays them on her lap.   [Place hands on lap.]

There's a Cobbler

There's a cobbler down our street
Mending shoes for little feet.
With a bang and a bang and a bang, bang, bang;
And a bang and a bang and a bang, bang, bang!

Mending shoes the whole day long,
Mending them to keep them strong,
With a bang and a bang and a bang, bang, bang;
And a bang and a bang and a bang, bang, bang!

The Policeman

The policeman walks with heavy tread,
Left, right, left, right.
He swings his arms, holds high his head,
Left, right, left, right.

The More We Get Together

The more we get together, together, to-

gether, the more we get to gether the

happier we'll be. For your friends are

my friends and my friends are your friends, the more

we get together the happier we'll be.

Frère Jacques

Frè-re Jac-ques, Frè-re Jac-ques,

Dor-mez vous? Dor-mez vous? Sonnez les ma-ti-nes

Sonnez les ma-ti-nes, Din, Din, Don; Din, Din, Don.

Are you sleeping? Are you sleeping,
Brother John, Brother John?
Morning bells are ringing, morning bells are ringing,
Ding, Ding, Dong; Ding, Ding, Dong.

92

Storybook Ideas

The Daddy Book, Robert Stewart (McGraw-Hill, 1972).

Doctors and Nurses, What Do They Do? Carla Greene (Childrens Press, 1963).

I Want to Be A Policeman, Carla Greene (Childrens Press, 1958).

My Friend the Babysitter, Jane W. Watson (Golden, 1971).

Grampa and Me, Patricia L. Gauch (Coward, McCann and Geoghegan, 1972).

I Want to Be A Farmer, Carla Greene (Childrens Press, 1959).

Feelings Between Brothers and Sisters, Marcia M. Conta and Maureen Reardon (Childrens Press, 1974).

Mothers Can Do Anything, Joe Lasher (Whitman, 1972).

Nobody Asked Me If I Wanted A Baby Sister, Martha Alexander (Dial, 1971).

I Want to Be A Fireman, Carla Greene (Childrens Press, 1959).

Helpers Who Work At Night, E. Hoffman (Capricorn, 1963).

Let's Find Out About the Hospital, E. Kay (Franklin Watts, 1971).

Daddies, What They Do All Day, Helen Puner (Lothrop, Lee and Shephard, 1946).

7

Discovering Our Environment

Enjoyment of their environment comes naturally to preschoolers. They are the first to delight over the spring dandelions appearing in the front yard, and they stand transfixed watching squirrels chase each other high in a tree. They are curious and always anxious to experience the realities of their surroundings. Joining hands to reach around a giant elm tree, smelling marigolds, touching the sticky pitch on a pine branch, tasting a fresh green onion, and listening to pounding rain on the garage roof are vivid sensual experiences that bring inquisitive youngsters into closer harmony with their environment. The outdoors is for fun. Leaves aren't just for raking, nor snow for shoveling; grass isn't just for mowing, and puddles certainly aren't there to be avoided!

Bringing nature indoors and reproducing it with rubbings, bouquets, pictures, and experiments delights children and stimulates questions. They want to know why things are as they are and they are glad to learn that they can have a part in preserving the beauty of nature.

Paper Work

Pollution Picture. Give each child a picture of an unspoiled outdoor scene and have him paste it to a piece of construction paper. Then let him paste gum and candy wrappers, tiny pieces of newspaper, bottle caps, and other such items on the picture. Caption the posters, "Don't Pollute." Talk about how beautiful the picture was before the pollution was added. Ask the children where pollution comes from. Does it come down from the clouds? Does it grow from seeds in the ground? Discuss with them how they can help keep nature beautiful.

Leaf Rubbings. Collect different kinds of leaves on a nature hike. Later, have each child place a leaf under a piece of typing paper and rub the flat side of a crayon over the paper. The shape of the leaf will appear on the paper. This works best when the leaf is upside down, making the veins more prominent. If the children enjoy doing these rubbings, suggest that they use other objects such as coins and keys.

Potato-Painting the Sky. To make a night and day sky, glue a half sheet of light blue construction paper to half of a black sheet of paper. The sun, moon, and stars can be printed on the day and night sky using potatoes and light yellow paint (use the recipe in appendix one, and add more yellow pigment for painting the sun). Prepare the potatoes in advance. To make the sun, cut a potato in half and dip the cut end in the paint. For rays, cut the other half of the potato down one-half inch, except for a narrow line extending across the diameter of the potato. For the moon and stars, draw the appropriate shapes on a cut potato, and again cut away one-half inch, except for the shape itself. Talk about the night and day sky as the children make their prints.

Snowflakes. Help each child fold a piece of typing paper in quarters, and let him snip off the point and cut designs into the paper. Tear along the edge so that the snowflake will be ragged and rounded. Holes can be added with a paper punch. When the paper is unfolded, it has become a snowflake.

Seed Pictures. Collect corn kernels, dried peas, or other good-sized seeds. On heavy paper letter words such as "corn" or "peas," or a child's name. Follow the words with glue, and let the children put the seeds on the lines of glue. For variety, draw daisies or sunflowers; the children can paste sunflower seeds in the center and outline the petals with corn kernels.

Book of Seasons. Save seasonal pictures from old calendars or greeting cards. Each child should have a picture for each of the four seasons, one for each page of his book. Using construction paper, draw or trace pictures of rakes, snow shovels, garden tools, beach balls, footballs, ice skates, and other objects that depict seasonal activities. Let the children match the objects with the seasonal pictures and paste them into their books. Title the book "My Book of Seasons," and staple the pages together. Encourage the children to talk about the seasonal activities they like best.

Imaginary Flower Garden. Cut out pictures of flowers from seed packages or magazines, and let the children "plant" their own gardens by pasting the cutouts on sheets of green construction paper. They could also "build" picket fences by pasting on white pointed strips of paper, and garden tools made from construction paper or cut from magazines could be added too. Discuss gardening, the use of each tool, and the necessity for weeding and watering gardens.

Fall Leaves. Collect a variety of bright colored fall leaves and press them in a book for a week or two. Let each child select his own leaves and glue them onto a sheet of heavy paper. You may want to add a small pine branch for variety. Talk about trees and how they change color in the fall, and how some trees stay green all year around.

Complete the Flowers. Draw a daisy by tracing around a quarter for the center and a nickel for the six petals. Draw a stem extending about three inches straight down and two leaves coming from the bottom of the stem. Go over the outline with a magic marker and use this model to trace four flowers on sheets of paper for each of the children. One of the flowers should be complete, but the others should be drawn with the stem, a leaf, or a petal omitted. Encourage the children to complete the missing parts and to color their flowers.

Seed Poster. Collect fruit and vegetable seeds, acorns, and pine cones. On construction paper draw or trace pictures of fruits, vegetables, and trees that grow from the seeds you have collected. When these pictures are cut out, the children can paste them on a large sheet of heavy paper and tape the appropriate seeds to them. Talk to the children about the cycle of little seeds growing into large trees that produce fruit which contains more seeds.

96

Crafts

Paper Plate Wall Hanging

Materials: paper plates
     crayons
     nature designs, magazine cutouts, or colored shapes
     dried leaves, weeds, flowers
     cord or yarn for hanging

Kids Do: Each child is given one and a half paper plates to color in autumn hues. He can then decorate his half plate by pasting some of the designs onto it. Glue the rims of the plates

together as shown; they may need to be reinforced with staples. String cord through a hole at the top for hanging.

The children bring their paper plate hangings on a nature hike, and fill the pocket with dried leaves, weeds, and flowers. Comment on the textures of the weeds and leaves. Why are some prickly? Why do dried leaves break? Compare freshly fallen leaves with dried ones. How do they feel different?

Miniature Fantasy Garden

Materials: toothpicks
     margarine tubs
     modeling clay
     popped popcorn, small corks, paper mint or medicine cups,
     heavy colored paper, small cutouts from magazines

Ahead of time: Cut flower or insect shapes from colored paper.

Kids Do: Each child makes flowers by sticking toothpicks into popcorn and corks and taping paper shapes onto them. Magazine cutouts may need to be glued to a paper backing before pasting to toothpicks. Stick toothpicks into mint cups and secure with tape. Plant the toothpick flowers and insects in a bed of modeling clay pressed inside the margarine tub.

Ask the children what each toothpick in their garden represents. Mention color, shape, size, and texture. Ask them what lives in a garden besides flowers. If they recognize the insects, mention that every garden needs insects so that flowers can bloom and grow. Use this project as an opportunity to go outside and explore life in a real garden.

Birdhouse or Bird Feeder

Materials: half-gallon milk cartons
    light cardboard, foil, or heavy paper
    paste-on decorations and/or colored paper
    ten-inch sticks
    cord or wire

Ahead of time: Cut a three inch hole in the carton as shown
    (1). Poke holes for the perch under the entrance hole and
    on the opposite side of the carton.

Kids Do: Each child decorates the roof and carton sides with
colored paper or nature designs and, with help, folds the cardboard in half to match the roof peak. The roof is then glued to
the top of the carton; staples can be used to reinforce it at the
top. Push a stick through the holes in each carton for a perch.
Thread wire or string through a hole punched at the top.

    Children will have fun picking a place in their yards for the
houses or feeders (see below). Let them help pick a spot in your

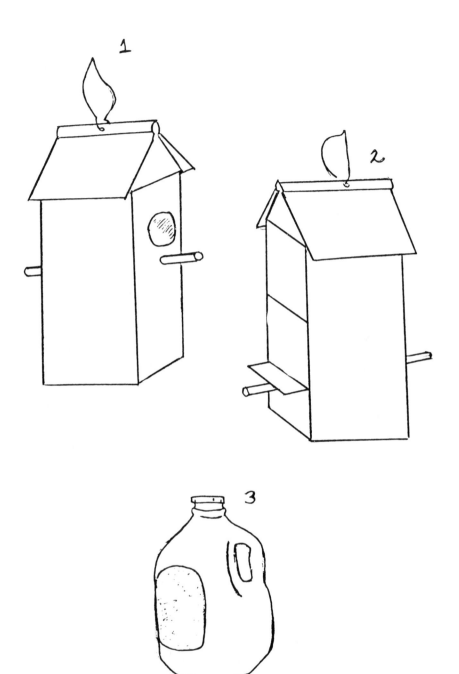

yard. Talk about the importance of helping nature's creatures. See if the kids know what birds eat, and what animals might compete for their food. They are playing a part in the balance of nature.

Bird feeders may be made by cutting cartons or gallon containers as shown (2 and 3). Decorate them as instructed for birdhouses.

Plant Peeper

Materials: heavy paper
    soda pop can
    ice cream sticks
    crayons or markers

Ahead of time: Trace a circle around the pop can and cut one for each child. Poke pin holes in the centers.

Kids Do: Each child decorates a stick and paper circle with crayons or markers and glues a popsicle stick to the circle as shown. Then he uses the handle to bring the circle close to his eyes and peeks through the pinhole with one eye to observe flowers, bugs, and leaves at close range. The "peeper" will make things appear larger.

Tiny Tree

Materials: medium-sized twigs with many branches
    colored paper

Ahead of time: Cut some squares, rectangles, triangles, or other recognizable shapes from colored paper. Leave some paper for the children to cut their own shapes.

Kids Do: Each child identifies different shapes of paper, cuts some designs with blunt scissors, and pokes them onto branches as shown. (Some will tear, so have extra paper on hand for repairs.) Children can take their trees home and

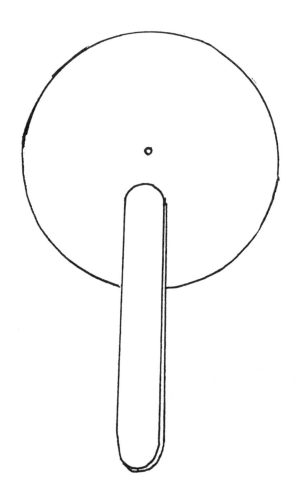

"plant" them in flower pots, or use them as wall hangings. Ask the kids what kinds of animals live in trees. Point out that the leaves of many trees don't stay on the year around. They fall off when the weather gets cold, and new ones appear in the spring. Why?

Tulips and Weeds

Materials: egg cartons
   bright paint
   pipe cleaners
   green, brown, or yellow kitchen sponges
   cottage cheese containers
   decorations for containers, green paper

Ahead of time: Cut cups from egg cartons. Cut sponges into ragged shapes for weeds. Cut pictures of garden tools or other decorations for the containers. Punch pinholes in the bottoms of the containers.

Kids Do: Each child paints his egg-cup "tulips" bright colors. When the paint dries, poke pipe-cleaner stems through the bottoms of the "flowers." Meanwhile, wrap pipe cleaners around sponges to make weeds. Decorate the containers with green paper and garden designs. As the kids plant their gardens in the containers by pushing stems into the pinholes, talk about gardening. Ask if they have seen weeds in gardens. Just what are weeds? Which do they like better, flowers or weeds? Why? How do gardeners get weeds out of gardens?

Pinwheel

Materials: eight-inch squares of paper
   markers or crayons
   thumbtacks
   dowel sticks

Ahead of time: Cut paper squares.

Kids Do: Each child decorates a paper square with crayons or markers. Cut slits diagonally from each corner half-way to the center, fold the four corners into the center as shown, and

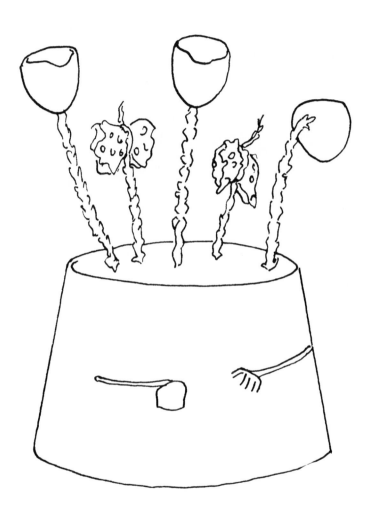

secure with a tack. Press the tack into the dowel stick. Blow!
Does the wind feel like the air coming from your mouth? How
do you know when the wind is blowing outside?

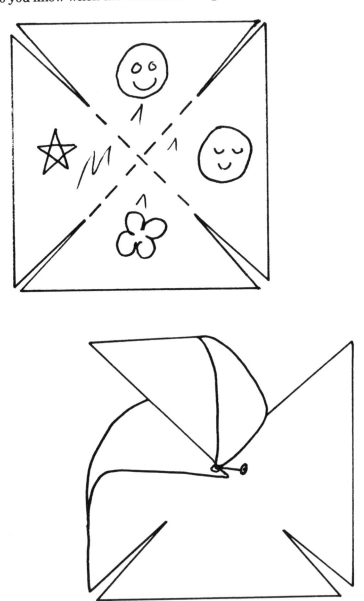

Activities

Celery in Colored Water. Place a stalk of celery in a glass of water. Add food coloring and watch the colored water travel up the celery stalk.

Magnet Fun. Children can have hours of enjoyment with a large magnet. Scatter items made from plastic, cloth, cardboard, and metal on your kitchen table, and let the children choose what they think the magnet can pick up. Walk through the house with them and have them point out certain things that they think the magnet will cling to, and then let them test it out.

Melting Snow. How many little ones know that melted snow is water? Place some snow in a cooking pan and put it on the stove to heat. The children will be amazed at how soon it turns to water, and then to steam if you let the water boil. Do the same with ice cubes that you have in your freezer. Talk about what happens to a lake when the weather is very cold and what happens to snow in the spring.

Green Potato Plant. Start your own indoor climbing vine with a white or sweet potato placed in a jar of water. Half of the potato should remain out of the water. Stick three toothpicks horizontally into the potato so that it will balance on the rim of the jar and be partly out of the water. Let the children help you start this project, and they will be surprised to see what has happened when they meet in your home again some weeks later.

Examining Plants. Let each child examine a leaf closely with a magnifying glass. The children will also be interested in looking at the intricacies of bark, moss, lichen, and flowers.

Weighing Fruits and Vegetables. This can be done with a kitchen scale or by balancing a small board on the back of a kitchen chair. If you are using a board, place oranges of equal weight on either end of your make-shift seesaw, and talk to the children about why it stays balanced. Have one of the children remove an orange. What happens? Try balancing two oranges

on one side and one on the other. Also experiment with two
bananas or an orange and a banana. Place a lightweight
stuffed animal on one side and an orange on the other. Why
does it tip to the side of the orange even though the animal is
bigger?

Indoor Gardening. Children enjoy planting an indoor garden
with seeds. Each child should have his own cut-down gallon
milk carton. Let them plant the seeds and water the soil. Sunflower and other fast growing seeds are suitable for this type of
gardening. The youngsters will be anxious to see what has
happened to their seeds when they return to your home for
school a few weeks later.

Charcoal Garden. This project can turn into an impressive spectacle, and the children can help you prepare it. You will need charcoal briquets, or small pieces of brick or coal, as well as small twigs and an aluminum pie plate. Mix up a solution made from the specified quantities of the following household products: six tablespoons each of salt, bluing, and water, and one tablespoon of ammonia. Put the charcoal in the pie plate. Apply glue to the twigs, attach them to the charcoal, and allow the glue to dry. Pour the liquid mixture over the coal and twigs. In a few hours crystals and florets will begin appearing. To give the garden more color and growth, add food coloring and more ammonia with a medicine dropper.

Wind Instruments. To test the wind, make a weather vane ahead of time, and choose a breezy day to demonstrate it. You will need a small, lightweight-cardboard triangle, about two inches on each side, a drinking straw, yarn for streamers, a straight pin, a bead or small button, and a pencil. Punch small holes at both ends of the straw and also in the middle. Attach the triangle to the straw with thread. Thread the streamers through the other side, and put a pin through the middle hole, then through the bead, and, finally, through the pencil eraser. When the vane is held in a breeze it spins rapidly.

On the day of the experiment, the children can make simple wind instruments of their own. These could include a pinwheel, a paper airplane, a balloon on a string, a small pennant of lightweight fabric attached to a stick, and a parachute paper napkin. (To make the parachute, tie a twelve-inch thread to each corner of the napkin. Tie the loose ends together and attach to a spool.) Each child should have an opportunity to demonstrate his wind instrument and to hold the vane.

Water Wheel. Water is an important source of energy. This can be demonstrated with a simple water wheel. You will need a one-gallon milk carton, four styrofoam cups, and a two-foot dowel stick. Open the top of the milk carton and cut out the bottom so that you have a box open at the top and bottom. Cut along the seams at two diagonally opposite corners and fold out the resulting pieces of waxed cardboard so that they are flat. Staple these pieces together, putting the seams at right angles to avoid bending. Trim off the corners to make a large circular shape. Staple four cups on the cardboard, as shown. For bal-

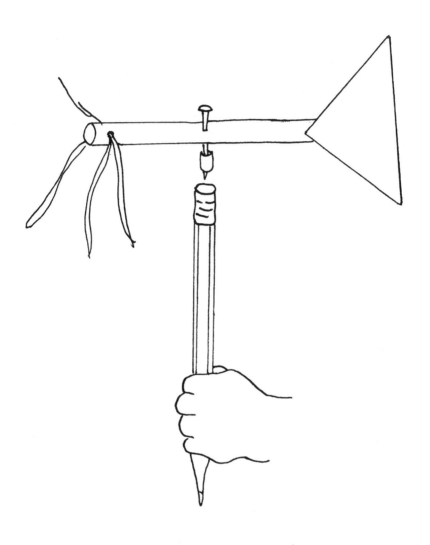

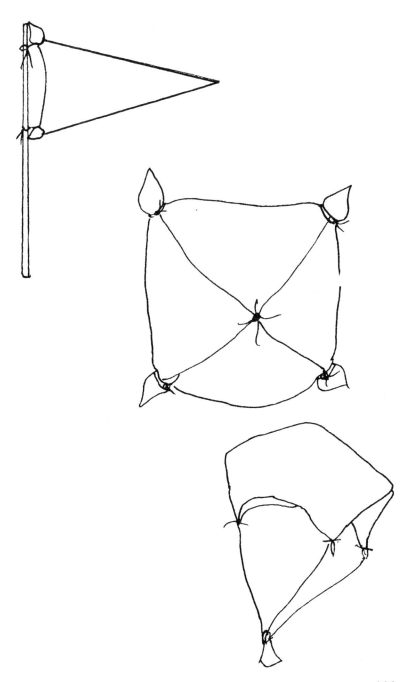

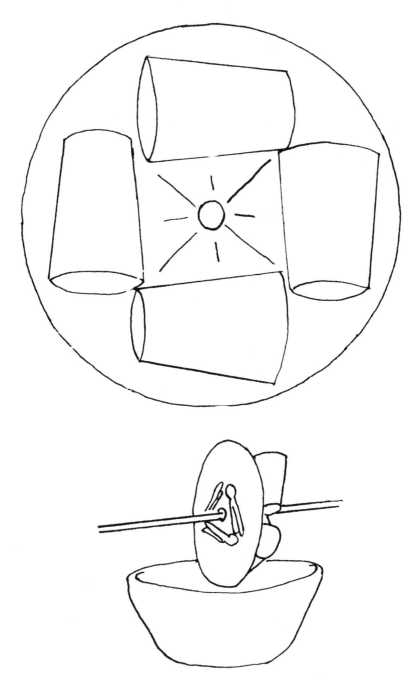

ance, you may want to glue or tape three round clothespins on the other side in a triangular shape. Punch a hole in the center of the circle and push the stick through the hole. The stick must fit loosely into the hole.

This activity is particularly suited for outdoors or in a laundry room. Two children should hold the stick, one at each end, suspending the water wheel over a large tub of water. A third child pours some water from a pitcher so that it falls into the cups attached to the wheel. This will make the wheel spin rapidly. Another child can collect water from the tub to add to that in the pitcher. The children should take turns doing different jobs.

Songs, Rhymes, and Fingerplay

Two Little Acorns

Way up high in the old oak tree,
Two little acorns smiled at me.
I shook the tree, and they fell down,
And then I picked them off the ground.

Star Light, Star Bright

Star light, star bright,
First star I see tonight.
I wish I may, I wish I might
Have this wish I wish tonight.

One Misty Moisty Morning

One misty moisty morning,
When cloudy was the day,
I chanced to meet an old man,
But I didn't know what to say.
He began to greet me,
And I began to grin.
How do you do? And how do you do?
And how do you do again?

March Winds

March winds and April showers
Soon will bring forth May flowers.

Mary, Mary, Quite Contrary

Mary, Mary, quite contrary,
How does your garden grow?
With silver bells and cockle shells
And pretty little maidens all in a row.

I Know a Little Pussy

I know a little pussy,
Her coat is silver gray;
She lives down in the meadow,
Not very far away.
Although she is a pussy,
She'll never be a cat,
For she's a pussy willow,
Now what do you think of that?

Five Little Leaves

Five little leaves so bright and gay
Were swinging on a tree one day.
A wind blew up and whirled around
Whooooooo . . . Whoooooo . . .
And one little leaf fell to the ground.

[Repeat with four little leaves, three little leaves, etc.]

Rain on the Green Grass

Rain on the green grass, rain on the tree,
Rain on the housetop, but not on me!

Oats, Peas, Beans

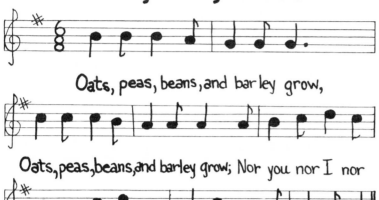

Oats, peas, beans, and barley grow,

Oats, peas, beans, and barley grow; Nor you nor I nor

any-one knows how oats, peas, beans, and barley grow.

Twinkle, Little Star

Twinkle, twinkle little star, how I wonder

what you are. Up above the world so high

like a diamond in the sky,

Storybook Ideas

The Day We Saw the Sun Come Up, Alice E. Goudey (Scribner's, 1961).

Where Does the Garbage Go? Paul Showers (Crowell, 1974).

The Storm Book, Charlotte Zolotow (Harper and Row, 1952).

Under the Trees and Through the Grass, Alvin Tresselt (Lothrop, Lee and Shepard, 1962).

Do You Know About Stars? Mae B. Freeman (Random House, 1970).

White Snow Bright Snow, Alvin Tresselt (Lothrop, Lee and Shephard, 1969).

A Fresh Look at Clouds, Richard Powers (Franklin Watts, 1964).

What is the Color of the Wide Wide World? Margaret Friskey (Childrens Press, 1973).

Rain Drop Splash, Alvin Tresselt (Lothrop, Lee and Shepard, 1969).

A Pocketful of Seasons, Doris Fostor (Lothrop, Lee and Shepard, 1961).

Down Come the Leaves, Henrietta Bancroft (Crowell, 1961).

Johnny Maple-Leaf, Alvin Tresselt (Lothrop, Lee and Shepard, 1961).

Water Is Wet, Sally Cartwright (Coward, McCann and Geoghegan, 1973).

Picture Book of the Sea, Jerome Meyer (Lothrop, Lee and Shepard, 1956).

8

Discovering Animal Life

Most children are naturally attracted to animals. Youngsters enjoy imitating the barking, purring, growling, and chirping of the creatures they so love, and acting out the hopping, snuggling, snuffling and wiggling actions of their own pets. Preschoolers love to watch animals that fly and buzz around them, and ones that slither through the grass, and frolic in parks and fields. They are fascinated to hear about exotic animals they have never seen, and delighted if they get to see such creatures on a zoo trip. They are interested in what animals eat, where they live, how they smell and how they feel. As you tell them about beasts, birds, fish and insects, they learn that animals are more than just movement and sound. Enjoying animals is not enough. Youngsters must also treat them properly. They should learn to handle puppies and kittens as the helpless babies they are. Preschoolers come to see these creatures as ones that eat, sleep, and need care just as they themselves do. Humane and careful treatment of pets and respect for wildlife result from this deeper understanding of the animals around them.

Paper Work

Crazy Zoo. From magazines or calendars cut out pictures (all approximately the same size) of various animals. Cut the pictures in half and have the children paste them on a sheet of paper to form "crazy" animals. Give the animals names such as

117

"categator," "zebraffe," "camelephant," and "chickodile." Encourage the children to make up their own names.

Fluffy Lambs. Make an outline of a mother sheep and two lambs on a sheet of construction paper, and let the children paste cotton balls to the forms. Tell the youngsters about how sheep are sheared and how the wool is used. Show them a garment that is made of wool.

Cookie-Cutter Tracing. Children enjoy tracing around forms, and cookie cutters are ideal for this. Let them create their own farm, while you discuss the importance of farm animals with them.

Animal Sponge Painting. Cut small simple shapes of animals from sponges. Let the youngsters dip the sponges in paint and make an imprint on a piece of typing paper. Keep each sponge form with a separate color of paint, so that each child is able to make a yellow cow, a green bird, and a red dog.

Stick Deer. Draw the torso, neck, and head of a deer on a piece of lightweight cardboard. Let the children collect small sticks in the yard to complete the animal: straight sticks for the legs, a short curved one for the tail, and ones with tiny branches for the antlers. Let the children tape the sticks on in the appropriate places with transparent tape. Talk to them about how animals such as deer, cattle, elk, and goats use their horns.

Blow Down the Bunnies. Draw three-inch bunnies on white paper. This can be done by drawing a small oval shape for the head and a large oval shape for the body and adding a little round tail, ears, whiskers, and other facial features. Leave a tab at the bottom of the body that can be folded back so the bunny stands up. The children can color or paint their bunnies, and then stand them up with the tabs and blow them over. Let them each have a turn at blowing all the bunnies down.

Crafts

Clothespin Butterfly

Materials: round clothespin
     heavy cardboard
     colored paper
     twist'ems

Ahead of time: Cut heavy cardboard in the shape of butterfly
    wings, as shown.

Kids Do: Tear or cut colored paper in small pieces. Each child
decorates his clothespin and wings with markers, paint or crayons. Glue colored paper onto wings. Help the children to push
the wings between the clothespin prongs so they wedge in
tightly. Wrap twist'ems around the "neck" and the lower prong
for antennae and legs. Talk about how delicate butterflies are,
and how children shouldn't pick them up or handle them.

WING

Potato Animals

Materials: potatoes
    broken popsicle sticks
    buttons
    pipe cleaners
    small pieces of heavy paper or felt
    raisins

Ahead of time: Cut paper or felt for pigs' and elephants' ears.

Kids Do: Let each child choose an animal to make and select a potato. For legs, use popsicle sticks. Pipe cleaners can be used as tails and elephants' trunks. Use buttons for pigs' noses and raisins for eyes. Glue other features on. Even making unrecognizable animals will be fun. Do all animals have eyes, ears, nose, and mouth? Do all have legs? The children will have fun naming their animals, and imitating their sounds. Which animals like to live with people? Which ones work for people?

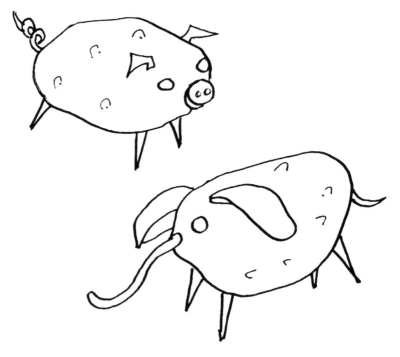

Egg-Carton Bugs and Caterpillars

Materials: egg cartons
    long pipecleaners
    short pipecleaners, straws, paper clips, twist'ems
    colored paper
    black crayon

Ahead of time: Cut egg cups from the cartons. For the caterpillars, punch a hole in the center of each of several cups. Leave some cups intact for individual bugs.

Kids Do: To make a caterpillar, each child bends a hook at one end of a long pipecleaner and pushes the other end through the holes in the egg cups. On the last egg cup, he can draw eyes. For individual bugs, add eyes to individual cups and glue on or stick in antennae and wings.

Ask the children what they think about insects. Ask if they know what these creatures do in nature. Ask if the pipecleaner feels anything like a real caterpillar. It is fun to combine this craft with a nature hike, looking for different kinds of insects and similar creatures.

121

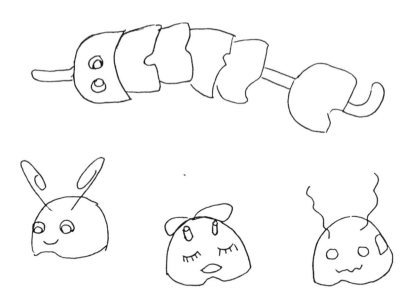

Folded-Paper Animals

Materials: two- and three-inch squares of heavy white paper
   small foil balls
   thin strips of stiff paper
   tape
   yarn
   cotton balls

Ahead of time: Cut little ears and feet.

Kids Do: Each child decides whether he will make a seal, a rabbit, a porcupine, or a mouse. The larger squares should be colored brown for the porcupines and seals, and the mouse and rabbit squares should remain white. Fold squares in half on the diagonal. For the mouse, draw eyes with a marker, glue on circular ears and feet, and glue the yarn under the paper for the tail (1). For the seal, fold up flippers, mark eyes, and tape the foil ball on the nose (2). For the porcupine, mark eyes, glue on circular feet, and glue on thin strips of paper for quills (3). For the rabbit, glue on ears, mark eyes, and glue on the cotton ball for the tail (4). Children can talk about where each animal lives, and what each animal eats. Then they would enjoy looking at an animal book to find pictures of the animals they have made.

122

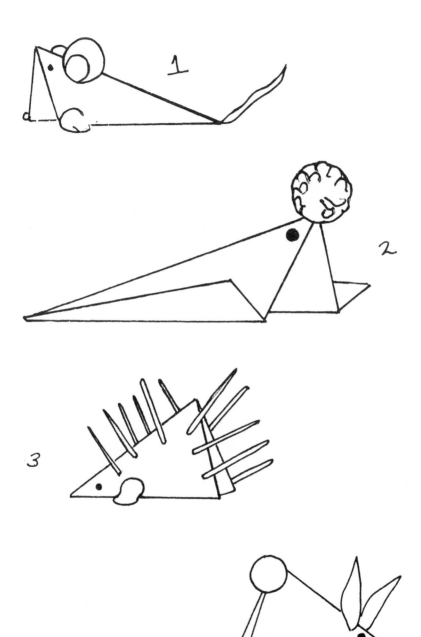

1

2

3

4

Hairy-Legged Spider

Materials: wooden thread spools
  black pipe cleaners
  colored paper
  egg carton cups
  paint
  sponge pieces

Ahead of time: Cut colored paper shapes for eyes, mouths, and
  hat brims.

Kids Do: Each child applies black paint to a spool with a
sponge piece. While the paint dries, talk about spiders, their
homes, webs, and activities. Sing "Itsy Bitsy Spider." When the
spool dries, glue on the features. Glue the hat brim to the top of
the spool, and glue the egg cup to finish the hat. Push the pipe-
cleaner legs into the hole at the bottom of the spool. Have the
children bend the legs into various positions. A string can be
tied around the spool so the spider dangles from its "web."

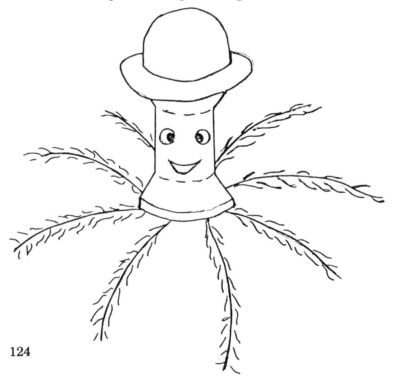

Tub Turtle

Materials: margarine tubs
    lightweight cardboard
    green paper
    egg-carton cups
    crayons

Ahead of time: Cut out cardboard feet and tail from the patterns shown. Cut out strips of green paper to cover the tub.

Kids Do: Each child glues the tabs for feet and tail to the inside of his tub so they will stick out as shown. He then colors in the eyes and mouth, and glues the head to the "body." Strips of paper can also be glued to the body, making the turtle look like a painted reptile. Ask the children where turtles live, and why they sometimes hide in their shells. Ask them if they ever feel like hiding under a box or in a closet, and mention how much fun it is to come out and surprise everyone.

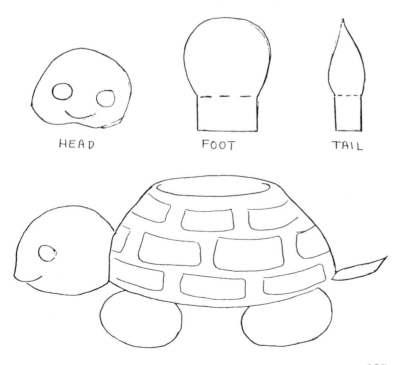

HEAD   FOOT   TAIL

125

Clothespin Zoo

Materials: lightweight cardboard
     animal pictures
     pincher clothespins

Ahead of time: Trace or draw animal shapes on cardboard and
     cut them out. Animals should be large enough to use cloth-
     espins as legs.

Kids Do: Each child colors an animal with markers or crayons
and attaches clothespins for legs. Which animals have four
legs, and which have only two? Which animals have wings?
Why? The children might enjoy constructing cages for their
animals from building blocks or small baking soda or food
boxes. What would they put in each cage for each animal to
eat?

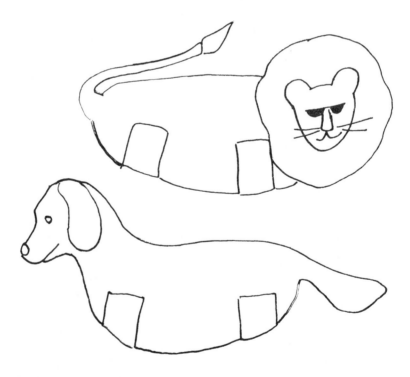

Spool Pets

Materials: spools
    lightweight cardboard
    crayons

Ahead of time: Draw simple designs of animal fronts and backs on the cardboard. Cut them out and mix them up.

Kids Do: Each child matches the front of an animal with a back. When he finds a match, he colors the pieces and glues them to the ends of a spool. Ask the children which of the animals they would like for pets. Why?

Activities

Fishing for Clothespins. Most young children enjoy this little game. Place several round wooden clothespins in a tub of water. Tie a string to a small pole and a nut or bolt to the end of the string. Then let each child see if he can get the string between the legs of the clothespin and pull out his catch.

Animal Cookies. Let the children help mix up the cookie dough from any simple cookie recipe, perhaps a favorite of your own. They will all want to have a turn at the rolling pin and will enjoy making their own animal shapes from cookie cutters. Let them do their own decorating with frosting as well as raisins, chocolate chips, coconut, and candies.

Fishbowl Anthill. If you are not squeamish about little crawling creatures, both you and the children will enjoy a fishbowl anthill. Sometime when you and your family are out for an afternoon hike along a lakeshore or in a wooded area, take along a small fishbowl. When you find an anthill, scoop some of the ants and sand into it. It is very interesting to watch how the ants tunnel alongside the glass and build up piles of sand at the entrances to their tunnels.

Squirrel Feeder. If you have trees in your yard, you will have no trouble attracting squirrels to a feeder during the winter months. The feeder can be a simple platform with low sides attached to a tree or to a railing. It should be located where it can be seen easily from a low window. Children enjoy watching the squirrels eat the corn and seeds and squeal with excitement when a bluejay swoops down for his share of the feast.

Examining Insects. Looking closely at lady beetles, ants, and other small insects through a magnifying glass is a learning experience for any youngster. Talk about the importance of insects and their different colors and sizes.

Field Trips. Besides nature hikes, there are all kinds of field-trip possibilities that relate to animals. Visiting a farm, a pet store, a zoo, or an animal hospital are just a few of these.

Elephant Trunk and Tail. If "Pin the Tail on the Donkey" seems too commonplace, try this activity for a variation. The children can help to make a large elephant from a cardboard box. Trace around a dinner plate for his head and ears, add a body and legs, and paint him. Cut six holes large enough for the end of your vacuum cleaner hose; one of these should be where the elephant's trunk belongs. Punch six smaller holes about the diameter of a pencil; one of these should be where the tail belongs. Some braided yarn attached to a pencil or short stick can serve as the tail. Each child is blindfolded in turn and tries to fit the trunk and tail into the proper holes. Encourage the children to feel the holes and tell if they are big ones for the trunk or little ones for the tail.

Animal Pretending. Imitating animal movements is fun, and it helps a child develop coordination. He can pretend he is a camel by walking on hands and feet (1). He can hop like a kangaroo (2), or flop like a seal (3). He can jump like a frog (4), or waddle like a duck (5). When he slithers like a snake (6), he can hiss and stick out his tongue. Doing the bunny hop requires him to squat, lean forward on his hands, draw his legs under him, and repeat the process, moving around the room (7). Children love clasping their arms straight in front of their noses, leaning over, and swinging their arms like an elephant's trunk (8). They can pretend to be geese by squatting, grabbing their shins, and walking forward (9). Or if they want to be flying birds, they can lie with their stomachs on the floor, lift their heads, and extend their arms and legs (10). To be a measuring worm, a child places hands and feet on the floor, knees straight, and takes small steps first with his hands and then with his feet (11). Encourage the children to make up their own animal movements, such as galloping like a horse, flapping their arms like a bird, or pouncing like a lion.

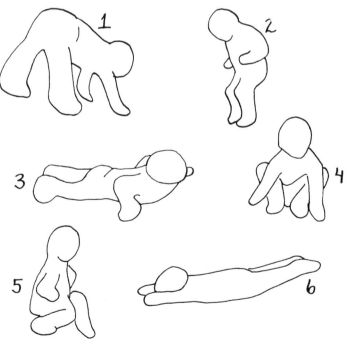

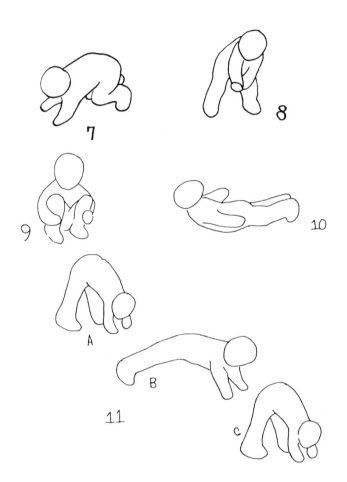

7

8

9

10

A

B

11

C

132

Shadow Menagerie. Encourage the children to perform an animal-shadow show on the wall. Demonstrate how to make different animal shadows, and let the youngsters do the rest. The eagle could fly over the alligator, who nips at the bunny's ear. Another bunny could hop into the scene, with a dog close at its heels. Let the children try different roles. Encourage them to invent their own techniques, projecting a spider, an octopus, or a wild-looking monster. This activity will not only stimulate their imaginations, but will improve their hand coordination.

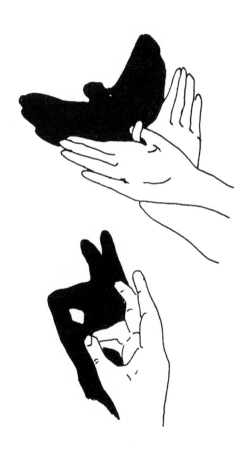

Songs, Rhymes, and Fingerplay

I Love Little Pussy

I love little pussy; her coat is so warm;
And if I don't hurt her, she'll do me no harm;
I'll cuddle and pet her and give her some food;
And pussy will love me because I am good.

The Cat and the Fiddle

Hey, diddle, diddle! The cat and the fiddle,
The cow jumped over the moon;
The little dog laughed to see such a sport,
And the dish ran away with the spoon.

Twiggy's Dog House [Use your own dog's name.]

This is Twiggy's dog house; [Bring tips of fingers together to make roof.]

This is Twiggy's bed; [Make motion of smoothing.]
Here is Twiggy's pan of food, [Cup hands together.]
So that she can be fed.
Twiggy has a collar, [Circle neck with forefingers and thumbs.]

With her name upon it, too.
Take a stick and throw it; [Make motion of throwing.]
And she'll bring it back to you.

Itsy Bitsy Spider

An itsy bitsy spider climbed up
   the water spout.   [Forefinger of left hand to
                                    right thumb; forefinger of right
                                    hand to left thumb. Keep
                                    alternating.]

Down came the rain and
   washed the spider out.   [Raise hands; wiggle fingers as
                                    you bring hands down.]

Out came the sun and dried up
   all the rain   [Make circle with arms over
                                    head.]

Then the itsy bitsy spider
   climbed up the spout again.   [Repeat action in first line.]

Baa, Baa, Black Sheep

Baa, baa, black sheep; have you any wool?
Yes, sir, yes, sir, three bags full.
One for my master, one for my dame,
And one for the little boy that lives in the lane.

Houses

Here is a nest for the robin,   [Cup both hands together.]
Here is a hive for the bee,   [Two fists together.]
Here is a hole for a bunny,   [Make circle with forefingers
                                    and thumbs.]
And here is a house for me.   [With fingertips together,
                                    make a roof.]

Walking Through the Jungle

Walking through the jungle,
What did I see?
A great big lion,
Roaring at me!

Walking through the jungle,
What did I see?
A little baby monkey,
Laughing at me!

Walking through the jungle,
What did I see?
A sneaky slippery snake,
Hissing at me!

[Encourage the children to make up their own verses.]

My Little Dog

Where, oh where has my little dog

gone? Oh, where, oh where can he be? With his

ears cut short and his tail cut long, oh

where, oh where can he be?

Donkey Song

Sweetly sings the donkey, at the break of day;

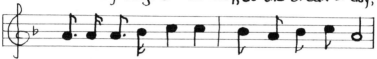

if you do not feed him, this is what he'll say,

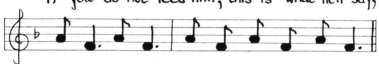

hee-haw, hee-haw, hee-haw, hee-haw, hee-haw.

Storybook Ideas

What Makes a Bird a Bird? May Garelick (Follett, 1969).
Animals Should Definitely Not Wear Clothing, Judi Barrett (Atheneum, 1970).
We Like Bugs, Gladys Conklin (Holiday House, 1962).
My Sea, illustrated by Hermann Foy (Hubbard Press, 1974).
Mousekin's Woodland Sleepers, Edna Miller (Prentice-Hall, 1970).

Birds in the Sky, Lucy and John Hawkinson (Childrens Press, 1965).

Benjy and the Barking Bird, Margaret B. Graham (Harper and Row, 1971).

The Way of an Ant, Kazue Minumura (Crowell, 1970).

The True Book of Farm Animals, John Lewellen (Childrens Press, 1954).

Seven Diving Ducks, Margaret Friskey (Childrens Press, 1965).

The Crocodile in the Tree, Roger Duvoisin (Knopf, 1973).

Animals in the Zoo, illustrated by Feodor Rojankovsky (Knopf, 1962).

Who Said Meow? Maria Polushkin (Crown, 1975).

I Like Caterpillars, Gladys Conklin (Holiday House, 1962).

A Book About Pandas, Ruth B. Gross (Dial, 1972).

Discovering Machines

Most young children are fascinated by machines, especially those with noisy engines, wheels, and lots of moving parts. In their play, children pretend they are driving cars and trucks, pushing lawn mowers, and using sewing machines. Machines play an important role in every child's dreams of the future. One day the youngster will be that brave firefighter speeding in a bright red fire engine to save a child from a burning building, or he will be the one who operates the controls of a dump truck or construction crane. While machines are an important part of a child's fancies, they are also vital to his real world. Most youngsters are eager to learn about the value and various uses of modern mechanical wonders. Visiting factories, railroad stations, service stations, construction sites, and airports illustrates the importance of machines and teaches safety rules that help the children to develop a genuine respect for the potential danger of those machines.

Paper Work

Crazy Machines. Give each child an assortment of items: various shapes cut from aluminum foil or fine sandpaper, ice cream sticks, string, buttons, bottle caps, wood screws, and small parts that can be found inside a broken transistor radio or clock. Let the youngsters tape or glue these items onto pieces of cardboard to make their own "crazy machines."

Machine Printing. Cut sponges into various shapes: circles, squares, rectangles, and triangles. Have the youngsters dip these sponges into paint and print the designs on heavy paper. Each child could start with a black rectangle, add red circles for wheels, and a half circle for a car top. They could also make sailboats with long rectangle bases and triangles for sails. Encourage them to create their own machine designs.

Machine Book. Staple together a three-page book for each child; title one page "Farm Machines," another "Road Machines," and the last "Home Machines." Cut out pictures from magazines and catalogs to represent the three categories. Help the children choose the pictures to be placed on each page.

ABC Machines. Sketch or trace simple forms of an airplane, a boat, and a car on sheets of typing paper. Identify each machine by printing the name next to it, beginning each word with a large capital letter. Let the children color the forms. Talk with them about machines that take people places. Can they name some more? Talk about letters and how they sound. What are some other words that start with *A, B,* and *C*?

Control Panel. Give each child a piece of cardboard that measures approximately twelve by fifteen inches. On the left side, have each child glue a colored-paper rectangle about the size of a light-switch plate. Then have him add two "push buttons" made from bottlecaps, buttons, or paper circles. Label one button ON and the other one OFF. Paper half circles representing speedometers can be glued to the center of the cardboard. Cut cardboard arrows to fit the half circles, attach them with paper fasteners, and letter SLOW on the left side of the half circle, and FAST on the right. Finally, on the right side of the cardboard attach "levers" by punching pipe cleaners through the cardboard and securing them on the back. The levers can be raised to an UP position and lowered to DOWN. The youngsters can use their panels to operate make-believe cars, robots, toys, or any machines they choose.

Machines Tell Time. Cut pictures from magazines and catalogs of various timepieces, including grandfather clocks, cuckoo clocks, alarm clocks, digital clocks, and watches. Let the children paste the pictures on paper and ask them to draw

140

lines under those people wear on their wrists, and circles around those that wake people up in the morning.

My Workroom. Cut out catalog pictures of stoves, refrigerators, dishwashers, washers, driers, and other large appliances. Let each child arrange his own kitchen or laundry room by gluing the pictures onto a piece of shelf paper. Smaller pictures of pots and pans or laundry aids can be pasted on top of the appliances. Ask the children what job each machine does. Which ones get hot? Which get cold? Why must you be careful not to touch the stove, or leave the refrigerator door open too long?

Crafts

Shoebox Train

Materials: shoeboxes, any size
 colored paper and other decorations
 string
 short sticks

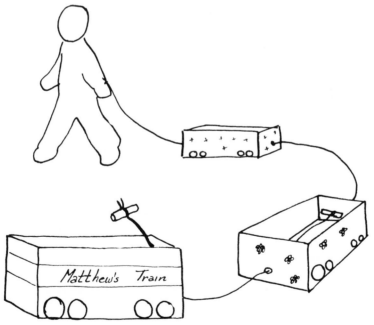

Ahead of time: Cut paper circles for wheels. Print each child's name on a strip of paper to paste on his train. Punch holes in the ends of the boxes for string.

Kids Do: Each child decorates three boxes with colored paper and pastes the circles on for wheels. Put the boxes aside, and before the next session, fasten them together. Push string through a hole in one of the boxes and tie the end inside the box to one of the sticks, as shown. Then push the string through the hole in the rear of the next box and tie it around another stick, as shown. Push the string out the front hole in the box. Repeat with a third box. The sticks will bump against the boxes, pulling them along. Children can pretend to be the engines for their little trains, whistling and chugging along. They can fill their boxcars with small toys after play, and make cleaning up more fun.

Paper Helicopter

Materials: typing paper
paper clips

Ahead of time: Cut pieces of paper, about two inches by five inches.

Kids Do: Each child decorates a piece of paper with crayons. Draw or paste a little person in a cockpit on one of the narrow ends, cut the paper, as indicated by the solid line, and fold the two tabs in opposite directions, as shown. Put the paper clip on the bottom end, as shown, and toss the spinner high into the air. The copter blades rotate as it falls. Tell the children there are special things a helicopter can do that a conventional airplane cannot, such as hovering, rising almost straight up, and coming straight down.

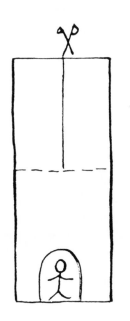

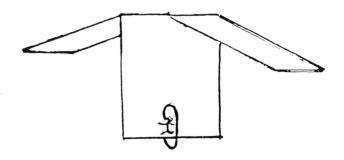

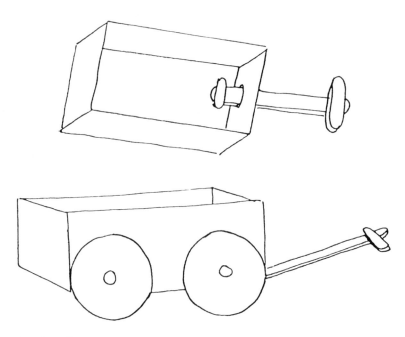

Donkey Cart

Materials: small stationery or greeting card boxes
    heavy cardboard circles
    paper fasteners
    ice cream sticks
    colored paper

Ahead of time: Cut a slit in the front of the box for the popsicle
    stick to fit in. Punch holes for the paper fasteners in the
    wheels and in the sides of the cart. Cut colored paper cir-
    cles to decorate the wheels.

Kids Do: Each child decorates his wheels and box with colored
paper and pushes an ice cream stick into the front slit. Glue a
smaller piece of stick onto each end, as shown. Help the children put the paper fasteners through the wheels and fasten
them to the carts. Will the cart go by itself, as some machines
do? Who usually pulls a cart or wagon? The children may have
some toy animals that can "pull" the carts and toy figures that
can ride in it.

144

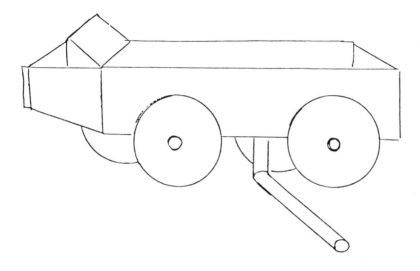

Fire Engine

Materials: milk cartons
     flexible straws
     plastic milk-bottle lids or circles of heavy cardboard
     dowel sticks

Ahead of time: Cut away most of one side of each milk carton, leaving a flap for the front windshield, as shown. Punch a small hole in the bottom for the straw. Punch holes in the bottlecaps or cardboard wheels for the dowel sticks.

Kids Do: Each child puts wheels on the ends of dowel sticks and tapes the sticks to the bottom of the truck. Rubber bands can be wound around the ends of the sticks to keep the wheels on. The children can push the straws into the bottom holes and take their trucks outside to play. They can put water into the trucks and let it flow out of the straw to douse some imaginary fire. If the children have seen real fire engines, let them share their experiences.

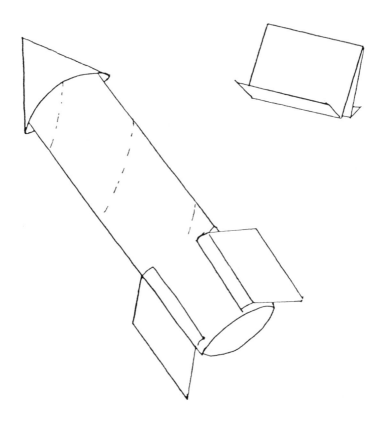

Rocket

Materials: paper-towel tubes
      three-by-five index cards

Ahead of time: Each rocket requires four index cards. Fold three in half and fold the ends up as shown; these will be the rocket fins. Cut the ends of the fourth to make a half circle. Staple this card to form a cone.

Kids Do: Each child puts glue around one end of his tube, and places the cone on it. He then glues the tabs of the fins near the bottom of the tube, as shown. Staples can be used for a firmer hold. The children can decorate their rockets and pretend to launch them into outer space.

146

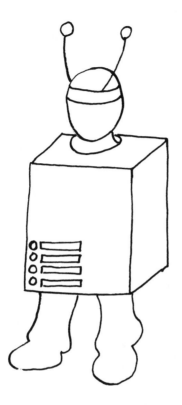

Robot

Materials: cardboard boxes large enough to fit over the children's bodies
strips of paper
bottlecaps
pipe cleaners
foil

Ahead of time: Letter such simple commands as STOP, WALK, SMILE, or CRY on the strips of paper. Cut a hole large enough for a child's head in the bottom of each box.

Kids Do: Each child decorates his box with bits of foil and tapes bottlecaps to the front of it for pushbuttons. Paste the

147

commands next to the buttons. For the headpiece, tape pipe cleaners to a strip of paper stapled to form a headband. The children can press each other's command buttons and see their fellow robots carry out their orders. Would they like to have a personal robot, or is it more fun to have human friends?

Activities

Machine Sounds. Tape record the sounds of various household machines such as a vacuum cleaner, a typewriter, a sewing machine, a lawn mower, an electric razor, an electric drill, and an electric mixer. Let the children listen to the sounds and try to identify them.

Garden Hose Roller Coaster. Place two garden hoses side by side several inches apart to make "tracks" for a large play ball. Start by placing the hoses straight and level, and ask the children to roll the ball down the tracks. Then curve the tracks and raise the outside edge of the curve slightly by sliding small sticks under the hose. Add hills to your curves by placing coffee cans or pieces of wood under the hoses. Talk to the children about roller coasters, trains, streetcars, and other vehicles that run on tracks. What makes a train stay on the tracks?

Acting Out Machines. Have the children take turns acting out various machines. To help them get started, suggest that they imitate cars by revving up the engine and squealing the brakes, airplanes by spreading their arms and buzzing about, motorcycles by stepping hard on the starter and twisting their hands to make the engine roar, irons by making the motions of ironing a garment, or electric razors by rubbing their faces and making a buzzing sound. Soon they will catch on and want to do imitations of their own choosing.

Working Machines. To demonstrate the necessity of machines and tools, show the children how different machines perform different functions. Show the youngsters how an auto jack works. First have them see if they can raise the back of the car up by lifting the back bumper. Then show them how easily it can be done by using a jack. Remove the jack from the car and let the children examine it closely. To demonstrate a machine that works faster than people show the children a mixer or blender. Let the children mix cake batter by hand, and then show them the speed with which a blender does the job. Point out that machines can be dangerous and explain why children should never plug an electric cord in by themselves. (CAUTION: These demonstrations should not be attempted unless at least one other adult is present to help supervise.)

Imaginary Machines. Encourage the children to use their imaginations to create machines that they would like to have. Suggest some of your own, such as one that, at the touch of a button, would clear the dirty dishes from the table and then wash, dry, and put them away, or another that would gobble up all the dirty, ragged, and torn clothing and send it back clean and good as new. Let each child have a turn at describing his own imaginary machine.

Playing Train. Have the youngsters line up, one behind another, and have each place his left hand on the left shoulder and his right hand on the right elbow of the child ahead of him. The children walk forward as they rotate their right arms to imitate the motion of the pistons on the wheels of the locomotive, and they toot their whistles as they go. Let them take turns being leader.

Field Trips. An outing requiring less preparation than those mentioned earlier could be a walk through your neighborhood to identify as many machines as possible.

Songs, Rhymes, and Fingerplay

Choo-Choo Train

This is a choo-choo train	[Bend arms at elbows.]
Puffing down the track.	[Rotate forearms in rhythm.]
Now it's going forward,	[Push rotating arms forward.]
Now it's going back.	[Pull rotating arms back.]
Now the bell is ringing	[Pull bell cord with closed fist.]
Now the whistle blows	[Hold fist near mouth and blow.]
What a lot of noise it makes	[Cover ears with hands.]
Everywhere it goes.	[Stretch out arms.]

149

The Car

Jump in the car;
Turn the key;
Shift the gear;
One, Two, Three.

Shift to high;
Shift to low;
Honk the horn;
And off we go.

[Have the children create their own motions.]

The Little Clock

There's a neat little clock;
In the schoolroom it stands.
And it points to the time
With its two little hands.

And may we, like the clock,
Keep a face clean and bright,
With hands ever ready
To do what is right.

Look at the Jet

Look at the jet
Way up in the sky,
Going so fast
And flying so high.

Up in the heavens
As far as can be,
I can see it,
But it can't see me.

Here Is the Engine

Here is the engine coming
   down the track;   [Hold up thumb.]
Here is the coal car, just in
   back;   [Hold up pointer finger.]
Here is the boxcar carrying
   the freight;   [Hold up middle finger.]
Here is the mail car. Don't
   be late!   [Hold up ring finger.]
Way back here at the end of
   the train   [Hold up little finger.]
Rides the caboose through the sun and the rain.

The Boats

This is the way, all the long day,
The boats go sailing by,
To and fro, in a row,
Under the bridge so high.

[Have the children use one hand as boat and the other as
bridge and move the boat back and forth under bridge.]

Down by the Station

Down by the station, early in the morning,

see the little puffer trains all in a row.

See the engine driver pull the little handle.

Choo, choo, choo and off we go.

152

The Bus

1. The wheels on the bus go round and round,

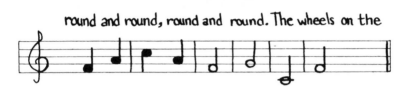

round and round, round and round. The wheels on the

bus go round and round, all day long.

2. The horn on the bus goes beep, beep, beep...

3. The windshield wipers go swish, swish, swish...

Storybook Ideas

The ABC of Cars, Trucks and Machines, Adelaide Hall (American Heritage Press, 1970).

The Giant Nursery Book of Things That Work, George J. Zaffo (Doubleday, 1967).

The Toolbox, Anne and Harlow Rockwell (Macmillan, 1971).

Clocks and More Clocks, Pat Hutchins (Macmillan, 1970).

Rockets and Satellites, Franklyn M. Branley (Crowell, 1970).

Bulldozers, Loaders, and Spreaders: A Book About Roadbuilding Machines, The Green Vale School (Doubleday, 1974).

The Big Book of Real Trains, Elizabeth Cameron (Grosset and Dunlap, 1972).

Mike Mulligan and His Steam Shovel, Virginia Burton (Houghton Mifflin, 1939).

Machines, Anne and Harlow Rockwell (Macmillan, 1972).

Mario's Mystery Machine, Sibyl Hancock (Putnam's, 1972).

The Great Big Car and Truck Book, Richard Scarry (Western, 1974).

Maybelle, the Cable Car, Virginia Burton (Houghton Mifflin, 1952).

10

Discovering the World of Make Believe

Fearsome giants bellow "Fe Fi Fo Fum," and dashing princes rescue helpless maidens in the world of make-believe. Children listen spellbound as Little Red Riding Hood innocently approaches her grandmother's door, and giggle at Rip Van Winkle who sleeps until birds nest in his beard. The grand adventures of Cinderella or Paul Bunyan and Babe the Blue Ox stretch a child's imagination and, at the same time, establish a lifelong attachment to the rewards of reading.

Paper Work

Real and Make-Believe. Divide a large sheet of paper into two sections, one entitled "Real" and the other entitled "Make-Believe." Cut pictures from children's magazines or make simple forms from construction paper of such things as witches, ghosts, magic wands, devils, monsters, and magic carpets. Mix these with pictures of real people, animals, buildings, and furniture. Let the children decide which are real and which are make-believe. Have them paste the pictures in the proper sections.

Three Little Pigs Poster. Pass out broomstraws, twigs, and small pebbles, and tell the story of the three pigs while the children paste and tape these materials in the outlines of three houses that you have drawn on a large piece of cardboard. Talk to the children about building materials. Which house would be the strongest? Why?

Fantasy Painting. Mix up a batch of fingerpaint using the recipe in appendix one. While the children are painting, ask them what kinds of things they would find in their own make-believe wonderland. Have them create their own imaginary figures and change them into different shapes, making up stories as they go along.

Hansel and Gretel Finger Puppets. Each child will need three finger puppets: Hansel, Gretel, and the old witch. Sketch a figure of a boy and girl on typing paper, each approximately two inches high, with the heads proportionately larger than the rest of the body; the witch, wearing a tall, pointed hat, can be somewhat larger. Leave tabs on either side of the figures, as shown. Cut the figures out, and let the children color them. Tape the tabs together to fit on the children's fingers. Help the children tell the story with their own visual aids.

Magic Coloring. Have the children make colored designs with crayons on typing paper. The coloring should be done heavily. When the first designs are completed, have the children color heavily over their creations with black crayon. Then they can use a blunt nail, ice cream stick, or their fingernails in random scribbling or in a design to gently scrape off some of the black, allowing the other colors to show through.

Funny Monsters. The children can each cut a large circle from colored paper and paste it on a sheet of heavy paper. Bits of yarn can be glued onto their monsters' bodies for fur, beads or buttons can be taped on for eyes, and sticks or drinking straws can be used for arms and legs. Encourage the children to think of other household scraps that might add other features to their monsters.

Modern Superheroes. Cut pictures of Superman, Spider-Man, Wonder Woman, and other children's favorites from discarded comic books. Also cut out pictures of buildings, cars, animals, and other items. Let the children paste the pictures in positions which show the heroes' superhuman abilities: Superman balancing a car on his head; Spider-Man scaling a skyscraper; and Wonder Woman riding an alligator. Are these figures real? Why is it fun to pretend that people can do these things?

Pot of Gold at the End of the Rainbow. Cut arched strips from rainbow-colored construction paper. Make circles three inches

in diameter from black construction paper, and cut them in half for the pots. Help the children glue them on the edges, and let them buckle outward, as a pocket. The children can stuff gold Christmas tinsel or yellow yarn in the pockets. Help them glue the rainbow colors in place, and ask them if they have ever seen a rainbow. Is there really a pot of gold at the end of one? Talk about the different colors in the rainbow, and discuss where and when rainbows can be found.

Crafts

Marble-Eating Monster

Materials: small round or rectangular kitchen boxes (salt, oatmeal, baking soda, rice, cake mix)
bottlecaps
colored paper

Ahead of time: Cut oval paper shapes for eyes. Seal the tops of the boxes with tape, and cut mouth-shaped holes at the bottom as shown.

Kids Do: Each child covers his box with colored paper. Strips of paper can be glued on for hair, and eyes and bottlecap noses can be added. Children enjoy rolling marbles or small balls toward the mouth opening trying to make the "monster" gobble up the marbles.

Royal Potato Family

Materials: four potatoes: two medium, two small
     felt
     yarn
     cotton
     paper

Ahead of time: Cut out crowns for the king, queen, princess, and prince potatoes. Cut paper or felt shapes for facial features.

Kids Do: The children decide which potatoes will be the king and queen and which will be the prince and princess. Glue on facial features. Tear some cotton and glue it on for the king's hair and beard. Use yarn or curled paper for the others' hair. Glue crowns together and place on the potato heads. What fairy tales do the children know that tell about kings and queens? Did they know that the prince and princess were the royal family's son and daughter? Show the children some pictures of royalty, and read them a fairy tale about princes and princesses.

Magic Wand

Materials: lightweight cardboard
    aluminum foil or glitter
    sticks

Ahead of time: Cut five-pointed stars from cardboard.

Kids Do: Each decorates his star with foil or glitter and tapes the star to a stick. Children can act out a fairy tale or pretend they have magic powers which make stuffed animals disappear under pillowcases or behind tables.

Giants and Elves

Materials: medium-sized paper bags large enough to fit over a
    child's head
    small lunch sacks
    colored paper

Ahead of time: Cut strips of paper for the giants' hair and
    eyebrows and green triangles for the elves' hats. Cut eyes,
    brows, noses, and long red tongues. Cut irregular white
    shapes for moustaches, beards, and hair.

Kids Do: Each cuts the bottom of his giant bag into strips for
the beard and pastes on paper hair. Holes are cut for eyes, and
eyebrows and nose are pasted on the bag. Children can put
their bags over their heads and pretend to be giants.

Glue paper features to the smaller bags as shown. The children can put their hands inside the bags and open and close the
mouth to make their elves talk. They can pretend to be both elf
and giant at once, with the giant holding the elf in his hand. Or
some children can be giants, and others can be elves.

Martian Baby Buggy

Materials: egg cartons
     drinking straws
     colored pipe cleaners
     wooden spools

Ahead of time: Cut four-inch sections of the ends of the carton
    lids. Cut the egg cups from the cartons.

Kids Do: Each tapes two four-inch lid ends together at right angles, as shown. He then passes a straw through a spool, centers the spool, and bends the straw up at each end where it is taped to the buggy. Repeat with the other roller assembly. A baby Martian can be made by decorating an egg cup with paper facial features and pipe-cleaner antennae. Children enjoy making up their own outer-space stories.

Humpty Dumpty

Materials: L'eggs pantyhose containers
    colored paper
    masking tape
    scraps of fabric

Ahead of time: Cut strips of paper for Humpty's base. Cut eye and mouth shapes from masking tape. Cut small strips of fabric for bow ties.

Kids Do: Each sticks eyes and mouth on his egg, colors them, and tapes a bow tie in the proper place. Form rings with the strips of paper and tape the ends together for the bases. Now

165

each child can place Humpty on a stand and see what happens when he is knocked off. He won't shatter like the fairy-tale Humpty, but he may split open in the middle.

Activities

Magic Mirror. Have one child stand in front of a make-believe mirror and act out various movements: combing hair, licking a lollipop, brushing teeth, putting on mittens. Another child faces him and pretends to be the mirror image, imitating every move.

Jack and the Beanstalk. Help the children act out the fairy tale "Jack and the Beanstalk." Give one child a handful of beans, and have him trade it for Jack's stuffed dog or other animal. Ask the children to pretend they are climbing a beanstalk. Hide a pantyhose egg, and let one child pretend he is the giant guarding the egg. The other children try to sneak it away from him and race toward the beanstalk and freedom. The youngsters will delight in saying "Fe Fi Fo Fum" in their "giant" voices.

Talking Animals. If animals could talk, what would they say? Use animal pictures, toys, or pets, and ask the children to make up conversations between animals.

Magic Carpet Ride. Have the children sit on throw rugs and pretend they are flying on magic carpets. What do they see from high in the sky? Where would they visit first?

Group Make-Up Story. The teacher makes up a story, letting the children take turns filling in words and phrases. The story might go as follows: "I was walking down the street when, all of a sudden, I saw a great big purple _____. I was so scared that I jumped into a _____ and broke my _____. Just then I looked up into the sky, and there flying right at me was a _____. It was coming so fast that. . . ." These stories can go on and on, and as the youngsters catch on, they take a greater part in telling them.

Pioneer Pretending. Take the children to a park or wooded area and tell them about how early pioneers lived in the wilderness. Help them find a sheltered place, spread their blanket, and pretend to build a fire. What would they eat? How would they keep warm at night? What would they do if a wild animal appeared? How would they build a house in the winter time? Talk to them about outdoor survival and the importance of staying close to their parents when they are in the woods.

Penny Magic. Even small children can enjoy doing very simple magic. To make a penny disappear from a glass, have the child place a penny in the palm of his hand and place a clear drinking glass over it so that the penny appears to be in the glass. He then shows it to his friends. (Actually, parents are a better audience. They're more gullible; friends catch on too fast.) To make the penny disappear, the child places a scarf or dish towel over the glass. As he says "Abracadabra" he clenches the penny in his fist and removes the scarf to display the empty glass.

Another penny trick that is fun for little ones involves turning two pennies into three. The child sticks a penny to clay and attaches it under the edge of the table while no one is looking. Then, with the other children watching, he places two pennies on the table. Pushing the pennies off the edge of the table into his hand, he at the same time lets the penny sticking to the clay fall into his hand. He clenches his fist, says "Abracadabra" and opens his hand to show three pennies. Talk to the youngsters about magicians and how they pretend to do things that don't really happen.

Flying Saucers. Take the children out into the yard and show them how to toss Frisbees. Let them try to catch the saucers as they land. Tell them about flying saucers, and help them imagine what people who might live on other planets would look like. Would they have one leg and three arms, or maybe two heads? Encourage them to imitate the actions of their make-believe spacemen. Have them make up some nonsense words to represent "outer-space talk."

Songs, Rhymes, and Fingerplay

If All the World

If all the world were apple pie,
And all the sea were ink,

168

And all the trees were bread and cheese,
What should we have to drink?

There Was a Crooked Man

There was a crooked man,
And he went a crooked mile.
He found a crooked sixpence
Against a crooked stile.
He bought a crooked cat
Which caught a crooked mouse;
And they all lived together
In a little crooked house.

Humpty Dumpty

Humpty Dumpty sat on a wall,
Humpty Dumpty had a great fall.
All the king's horses
And all the king's men
Couldn't put Humpty together again.

There Is a Purple Monster

There is a purple monster,
That lives down the street;
His teeth are red, his eyes bulge out,
And warts grow on his feet.

He growls and roars and hisses
As loud as he can be,
Frightening all the children,
And even scaring me.

Wee Willie Winkie

Wee Willie Winkie runs through the town,
Upstairs and downstairs in his nightgown.
Tapping at the window, crying at the lock:
"Are the children in their beds, for now it's nine o'clock?"

Tall and Small

Here is a giant who is tall,
    tall, tall;   [Children stand tall.]
Here is an elf who is small,
    small, small;   [Children slowly sink to floor.]
The elf who is small will try,
    try, try   [Children slowly rise.]
To reach to the giant who is
    high, high, high.   [Children stand tall and
                          stretch their arms.]

Giants and Fairies

We are giants great and strong;
watch us as we stomp along. Fairies dancing
to and fro, lightly stepping on tiptoe.
Giants tall, fairies small.

A Tiny Elf

A tiny elf I once did see, and

in my dreams he sang for me. He skipped and danced and

twirled around, but when I woke he couldn't be found.

Storybook Ideas

The Strange Story of the Frog Who Became a Prince, Elinor L. Horwitz (Delacorte, 1971).

Giants Indeed!, Virginia Kahl (Scribner's, 1974).

The Shoemaker and the Elves, the Brothers Grimm (Scribner's, 1960).

Jimmy and Joe Find a Ghost, Sally Glendinning (Garrard, 1969).

The Little Red Hen, Paul Galdone (Seabury, 1971).

Mystery of the Magic Meadow, Margaret Friskey (Childrens Press, 1968).

Snow-White and the Seven Dwarfs, the Brothers Grimm (Farrar, Straus and Giroux, 1972).

The Witch, the Cat, and the Baseball Bat, Syd Hoff (Grosset and Dunlap, 1968).

Obedient Jack: An Old Tale, Paul Galdone (Franklin Watts, 1971).

The Hedgehog and the Hare, the Brothers Grimm (World, 1969).

Humbug Witch, Lorna Balican (Abingdon, 1965).

Rumpelstiltskin, the Brothers Grimm (Harcourt, Brace and World, 1967).

How Droofus the Dragon Lost His Head, Bill Peet (Houghton Mifflin, 1971).

11

Discovering Holidays

Jack-o'-lanterns, turkey gobblers, Christmas trimmings, Valentines, and Easter bunnies are all part of the seasonal festivities and fun that add sparkle to little eyes. Children love to take part in holiday activities. Pint-sized witches and ghosts giggle as they scare each other as well as themselves at Halloween parties. At Thanksgiving children learn about the Pilgrims, gratefulness, and gobblers, and they enjoy telling about their own big birds waiting to be stuffed and roasted. Christmas is an especially exciting time for little ones. Activities such as setting up a miniature Nativity scene, baking gingerbread cookies, or making simple tree ornaments to bring home add to their joy. Though holidays are usually celebrated as family days, they also provide meaningful opportunities for little ones to relate to their friends by exchanging gifts and Valentines. Through all these activities children learn the special significance of each holiday season.

Paper Work

Halloween Pumpkins. Give each of the children an orange sheet of construction paper. Have them trace around a pie plate, and help them cut their circles. Cut yellow triangles, circles, and crescent shapes for the eyes, nose, and mouth, and let the youngsters paste these on their pumpkins. Cut out green stems for each child to paste on the top.

Horn of Plenty. Draw a large cone with a curved "tail" and an opening at least eight inches high. The children can paste pictures of foods they like in the opening. What kinds of foods did the Pilgrims eat? Why were they so thankful?

Santa Claus Mask. Cut ovals of heavy paper about the size of a child's face and have the children color them pink. Cut holes for eyes. Attach triangles of white paper to the chins, and let the children glue on cotton balls for beards. Add floppy red hats of felt or construction paper trimmed with cotton balls. Measure elastic lengths to fit half way around the children's heads and staple them to the mask. Encourage the youngsters to play Santa's helpers while they pretend to make toys and load them onto a sleigh.

Greeting Cards. Pass out several card-size pieces of heavy paper to each child. Drop some tempera paint on each child's paper, and have the youngsters blow gently through straws to make designs with the paint. When the children are finished with their first card, they can set it aside to dry and make another with a different color paint. Another color can be added to each card when the first color is dry. Fold the cards, and ask the children what greeting they would like you to print inside.

Valentine Placemats. Cut out various sizes of hearts from red construction paper. Give each child a paper white lace placemat or a large sheet of white construction paper, and let them paste on some hearts. They can repeat this for each member of their family, with an identifying name on each mat. Encourage the children to take their placemats home to be used for a special Valentine dinner.

Shamrock Painting. Trace the shape of a shamrock on a heavy sheet of paper for each child. Mix up green paint from the recipe in appendix one, and let each child paint his shamrock by using small sponges or cotton balls.

Easter Baskets. Cut two half circles from light brown construction paper for each child. Staple the rounded edges together to form an envelope "basket" with the top left open. Cut thin strips of paper ten inches long and attach as handles. The children can glue various colors of Easter-egg shapes to the outside of their baskets and stuff Easter grass on the inside.

Birthday Hats. Help the children make cone-shaped hats from pieces of construction paper and give them each strips of colored paper to paste on the hat. Strings may be attached for ties.

American Flag. Make American flags for Washington's and Lincoln's birthdays or for Memorial Day. For each flag, cut seven red strips of paper, five-eighths of an inch wide and eleven inches long. Have the children paste these horizontally at intervals on a sheet of white typing paper. Cut squares of blue paper for the children to paste on the upper left-hand corners of their flags. They can stick some gummed stars on the blue field. Let the children tape their flags to sticks and march around with them. At a parade or at an athletic event, or whenever the American flag appears, people stand and remain quiet as it passes. Why?

Crafts

Witch Hat and Broom

Materials: black construction paper
old broom handles or sticks about three feet long

Ahead of time: Make cones for witches' hats from black construction paper. Cut broom handles to correct length.

Kids Do: Each cuts some newspaper into strips twelve to eighteen inches long. Put glue around the broomstick about four inches from one end and press the paper strips onto the glue so they hang down to form the "straw" of the broom. String can be wound tightly around the straw to hold it more securely to the broomstick. Children can wear their hats and ride their brooms around the room. What do witches do? Are they scary? Or are they an enjoyable part of Halloween make-believe?

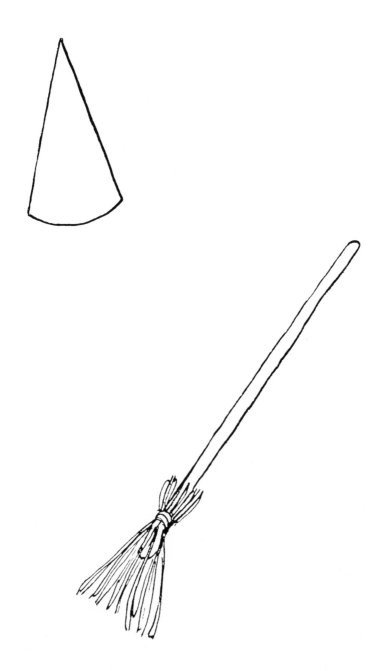

Paper-Plate Turkey

Materials: paper plates
colored paper

Ahead of time: Cut six-inch strips of colored paper, about a half-inch wide. Cut shapes of turkey head and feet as shown.

Kids Do: Each colors the bottoms of two paper plates brown and glues the head and feet in position on the uncolored side of one plate. The "feather" strips are then folded in half and glued around the top of the plate. The second plate is stapled to the back of the first one, with the colored paper features appearing between the two plates. The children like to imitate turkey sounds. Ask them what they're having for Thanksgiving dinner. Do they always remember to say "Thank you" for the nice things people do for them?

Holiday Candles

Materials: cardboard tubes of various sizes
lightweight cardboard
colored paper and small decorations
small pipe-cleaner pieces

Ahead of time: Cut flame shapes from colored paper. Cut small circles from cardboard to fit into the ends of the tubes.

Kids Do: Each tapes a pipe-cleaner piece to the bottom of a flame, glues a small circle inside his tube, and sticks the flame into the circle. He then can decorate the outside of his candle with colored paper or other small designs. Perhaps some real candles can be brought out and the children could be asked what happens to the flame when they blow very softly or very hard. Why should children be careful not to touch the flame or knock over a candle?

Jingle Bells

Materials: styrofoam cups
    ribbon or yarn
    old foil, wrapping paper, seals or tags
    glitter (optional)
    jingle bells

Ahead of time: Punch holes for ribbon in the bottoms of the cups.

Kids Do: Each cuts or tears foil, wrapping paper, or ribbon into small pieces and glues them to two cups. Glitter can be added. String a jingle bell on an eight inch length of ribbon. Pass both ends of the ribbon through the cup holes from the inside, leaving the bell inside and tying the ribbon on the outside of the cup into loops for tiny hands to hold. When the glue dries, sing "Jingle Bells" while the children shake their bells.

Christmas Tree

Materials: heavy green paper
   cardboard tubes
   small decorations: macaroni, popcorn, gummed stars, Christmas seals, pieces of ribbon, or wrapping paper
   tape

Ahead of time: Cut green half circles ten inches in diameter, shape them into cones, and staple.

Kids Do: Each decorates his tree. Tape two stars together back to back, and tape the ornament on the "treetop." When the glue is dry, place each decorated tree on top of its trunk, the cardboard tube. Ask the children if they are going to help decorate their own trees at home. Why are homemade ornaments and decorations so special?

Valentine Centerpiece

Materials: drinking straws
   red and white paper
   styrofoam cups

Ahead of time: Cut several red and white heart shapes from heavy paper. Punch holes in the bottom of the cups for the straws.

Kids Do: Each pastes small red hearts on his cup. He then tapes small white hearts onto large red hearts, tapes the large hearts to the ends of the straws, and pushes the straws into the holes in the cups. The children can use the cups as centerpieces for their Valentine's Day dinner. Let them also frost heart-shaped cookies for Valentine treats, and teach them a little Valentine song.

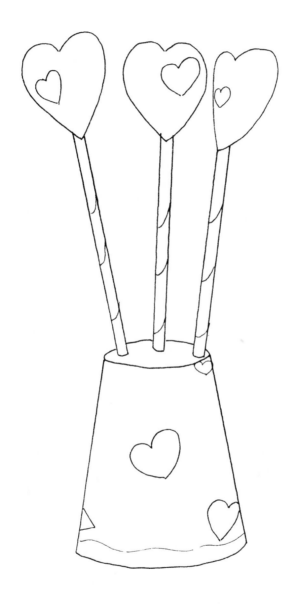

Paper Bunny

Materials: heavy white paper
uncooked spaghetti

Ahead of time: Cut half circles ten inches in diameter, form them into cones and staple them. Cut out ears as shown, and cut a hole in the middle to slip over the top of the cone. Cut circles for the eyes and noses. Make pinholes for whiskers.

Kids Do: Each child colors his bunny's eyes and nose, and pushes spaghetti through the holes in the cone for whiskers. He can draw toes or ovals for feet and slip the ears over the top of the cone. Rest the bunnies on little Easter baskets made from the bottom halves of milk cartons, with handles cut from the rest of the carton and stapled on. The children can cut strips of green paper to use for grass in their baskets.

Easter Duck

Materials: cardboard tubes, half wider than the others
heavy yellow and orange paper

Ahead of time: Cut orange diamonds for eyes and beaks and cut webbed feet as shown. Cut the narrow tubes into two- or three-inch lengths and the wider ones into four-inch lengths. Cut yellow paper into sheets large enough to cover the tubes.

Kids Do: Each glues the yellow sheets onto two tubes, staples or tapes the tubes together, and glues eyes, beak, and feet in the proper spots. What do ducks and chicks have to do with Easter? Do they both come from eggs? Let the duck ride in the Easter basket with the paper bunny.

Activities

Carving a Jack-o'-Lantern. Let the children help carve a pumpkin into a jack-o'-lantern. Allow them to decide where the facial features should go, and let them help draw them on with a magic marker. Let the children remove the seeds. After you have done the carving, they can help secure the candle. Sautéed pumpkin seeds make a delicious snack.

Pilgrims' Thanksgiving Feast. With the children's help, plan and prepare a Thanksgiving feast of raw garden vegetables, fruits, and nuts. Seat the children on the floor and, after a Thanksgiving prayer, let them share the food with each other.

Gingerbread Cookies. Children enjoy helping in the kitchen, and making gingerbread cookies to take home is a holiday treat. Use your own recipe or the one in appendix one, and let the youngsters have a part in sifting and stirring the ingredients as well as in cutting out their own gingerbread men. Show them how to put on the frosting with their fingers, and let them decorate their men with chocolate chips and raisins.

186

Christmas Angels. With the children dressed in snowsuits and boots, take them out in your yard and let them make angels in fresh-fallen snow. If the snow is several inches deep, they will enjoy falling backwards into it, moving their arms up and down for wings and spreading their legs for a skirt.

Easter Egg Fun. Dyeing hard-boiled eggs is an activity that even little children can enjoy. Help them paste rabbit ears or have them draw happy faces on their eggs. Set the eggs on paper cones, the ends of which have been cut off an inch or so from the point. Easter egg hunts are also easy to plan. If the weather is nice, hide some candy eggs out in your yard and let the children search for them.

Holiday Party Ideas. Costume parties are always fun at Halloween. Homemade costumes are often more original than manufactured ones. A sheet for a ghost, old clothes for a bum or scarecrow, and cardboard boxes for a robot are all simple ideas. A Christmas gift-exchange party is always exciting. Youngsters enjoy shopping for and picking out the gifts themselves. All party games should be noncompetitive; each little one should go home with a treat.

Field Trips. During holiday seasons many shopping malls offer free entertainment for children, and libraries sometimes have special programs. Visiting a pumpkin farm at Halloween or a Christmas tree farm at Christmas can usually be easily arranged.

Rhymes and Finger Play

My Jack-o'-Lantern

Out in the garden,
Clinging to a vine,
I found a fat pumpkin,
Waiting to be mine.

I carved out a face
And put in a light,
And then I had a jack-o'-lantern
Smiling bright.

Halloween

Ugly old witches flying on brooms,
Goblins and ghosts coming out of tombs,
Spooky haunted houses filled with bats,
Jack-o'lanterns, trick-or-treat, and scary black cats.

Thanksgiving Day

The harvest time is over,
Thanksgiving day is here;
We're thankful for so many things
This special time of year.

Little Jack Horner

Little Jack Horner
Sat in a corner
Eating his Christmas pie;
He put in his thumb,
And pulled out a plum,
And said: "Oh, what a good boy am I!"

Here Is the Chimney

Here is the chimney,   [Make fist, enclosing thumb.]
Here is the top,   [Place palm of other hand on
                              top of fist.]
Open the lid,   [Remove top hand quickly.]
And out Santa will pop.   [Pop up thumb.]

I Made a Little Valentine

I made a little Valentine,
My very first one,
And gave it to Mommy,
And oh, it was fun.

I made another Valentine,
Which added up to two,
And gave it to Daddy,
And said "I love you."

I made just one more Valentine,
Which came to number three,
It's for all the little girls and boys,
Who are so nice to me.

Jesus Died on Calvary

Jesus died on Calvary
For little children just like me,
But in the grave He did not stay,
He rose again on Easter Day.

This Little Bunny

This little bunny has two pink eyes;
This little bunny is very wise;
This little bunny is soft as silk;
This little bunny is white as milk;
This little bunny nibbles away
At cabbage and carrots all the day.

[Point to fingers or toes with each bunny.]

America Is Where I Live

America is where I live;
America is where I love;
My state is _____;
My town is _____;
But my country is America.

Storybook Ideas

The Halloween Pumpkin, Pamela Oldfield (Childrens Press, 1976).

Gunhilde and the Halloween Spell, Virginia Kahl (Scribner's, 1972).

Little Bear's Thanksgiving, Janice (Lothrop, Lee and Shepard, 1967).

The Silver Christmas Tree, Pat Hutchins (Macmillan, 1974).

Plum Pudding for Christmas, Virginia Kahl (Scribner's, 1956).

The Holy Night, Aurel von Juchen (Atheneum, 1968).

The Mole Family's Christmas, Russell Hoban (Parents' Magazine Press, 1969).

Christmas Eve, Edith Thatcher Hurd (Harper and Row, 1962).

Paddy's Christmas, Helen A. Monsell (Knopf, 1942).

Little Bear's New Year's Party, Janice (Lothrop, Lee and Shepard, 1967).

Miss Flora McFlinsey's Valentine, Mariana (Lothrop, Lee and Shepard, 1962).

Valentine Cat, Robert Bolla (Crowell, 1959).

Easter Treat, Roger Duvoisin (Knopf, 1954).

The Adventures of Egbert the Easter Egg, Richard Armour (McGraw-Hill, 1965).

12

Discovering Learning Skills

At the early age of three or four children are beginning to recognize and identify supermarkets by "reading" the large letters on the store signs. While they're not ready to read the package labels, they can distinguish differences among cereal boxes and identify some of the letters on them. Learning skills include more than memorizing the alphabet and numbers. They involve thinking, following directions, and recognizing likenesses and differences. As a child learns to identify rectangles, triangles, and circles, he is not only preparing to recognize different letters and words, but he is also gaining a better understanding of the shapes of things in the world around him. Learning to draw straight lines, circles, and other shapes gives the youngster practice in coordination that will later help him write his own name. Little children enjoy learning to sing the alphabet song, to recognize their printed names, to count on their fingers, and to identify shapes and colors. The more fun they have, the more they will look forward to future learning challenges.

Paper Work

Completing Shapes. Cut a number of sets of large circles, squares, rectangles, and triangles from colored paper. Paste one set of them on a large sheet of shelf paper for all the children to see. Cut the remaining shapes in half and help each child paste one-half of each shape on a piece of paper. Distribute the remaining halves so that each child has a set. Demonstrate how each shape should be completed, and ask the children to complete their own sets of shapes by placing the unpasted halves in the correct places. When the children have become proficient at this, the same procedure can be followed with the alphabet.

Using a Ruler. Give each child a ruler, colored pencils, and paper. Show each one how to draw a straight line using the edge of his ruler. When the children master drawing straight lines at different angles, encourage them to join the lines to form crosses, rectangles, squares, triangles and other figures.

Alphabet Word Pictures. Cut pictures of easily identifiable objects, including various toys, animals, foods, and furniture, from magazines or catalogs. Trace the letters of the alphabet on sheets of typing paper and cut them out. Let the children paste the pictures on a large sheet of construction paper. Then help them choose the first letter of the word which identifies each picture; the letters can be pasted above the pictures they symbolize. Over the course of the school year a number of these papers can be completed and brought out as memory games from time to time.

Alphabet Man. Let the children have fun with the alphabet. Trace and cut out the letters *V, M, O,* and *C* from construction paper. Give each child a set of letters and demonstrate how the letters can be arranged to form the figure of a man. Turn the *V* upside down for the legs; use the *M* for the trunk and arms, the *O* for the head, and the *C* turned sideways for a hat. Help each child paste his man to a sheet of typing paper.

Stair Steps. Give each child six strips of colored paper cut into one-, two-, three-, four-, five-, and six-inch lengths. Have them arrange the strips on a sheet of paper from the largest to the smallest and glue them on the paper. Ask the children to "climb the stairs" with their fingers, counting them as they go.

Tracing Practice. Give each child some heavy paper with penciled designs on it. These designs could include simple animal figures, squares, circles, and triangles. Remember, little hands are unskilled at very small movements, so make your figures quite large. The children can trace over the designs with crayons or felt markers.

192

Large and Small Circles. Give the children several round objects of varying sizes, from jar lids to quarters and nickels. Let them trace around the objects to make circles of different sizes. Let them color their circles, and have them tell you which is the largest, which the smallest, and which in between.

Days of the Week Wheel. Trace circles around a small pie plate on two different colors of construction paper and cut them out. Divide one of the circles into seven even sections, as though you were cutting a pie. Print a day of the week horizontally on each section, in order around the circle. From the second circle, cut out one pie-shaped section of the same size, ending your cuts just before the center, so you can punch a hole in the middle. Fasten the circles together at the center with a paper fastener, with the days-of-the-week circle face up on the bottom. Letter DAYS OF THE WEEK on the top circle and rotate the wheel as the children repeat the days of the week. As they grow familiar with the wheel, other games can be developed from it . . .Who knows what day of the week this is? Can you find it on our wheel? If today is Thursday, what will tomorrow be?

Number Squares. Divide pieces of paper into four square sections labeled *1, 2, 3,* and *4.* Give the children gummed stars or seals, or let them use colored paper designs with paste. Have them glue one triangle in section 1, two circles in section 2, three stars in section 3, and four apples in section 4. Have them practice counting the items and identifying the numbers. After they have learned these numbers, let them try the exercise with higher numbers.

Crafts

Pencil Holder

Materials: modeling compound (see Appendix One)
    paint (optional)
    pencils

Kids Do: Each forms his clay into a shape with a somewhat flat bottom and punches deep holes in it with a pencil. Allow it to dry according to recipe directions, and it then can be painted, if desired. The children can keep pencils and crayons in their creations and use them as paperweights or desk decorations.

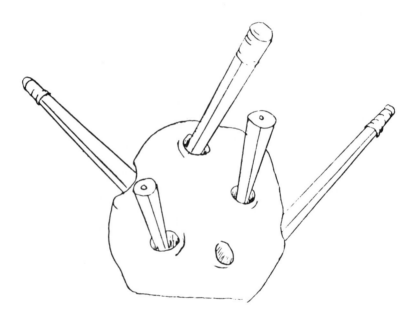

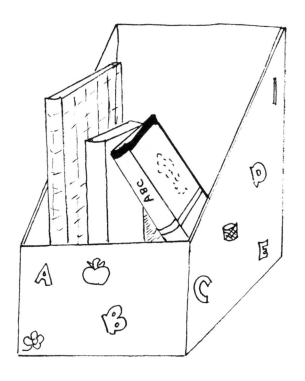

Bookcase

Materials: large cardboard boxes
  cutouts from magazines, wrapping paper, or other colored-paper designs

Ahead of time: Cut away part of the boxes' fronts and sides, as shown.

Kids Do: Each paints his box and decorates it with colored designs. Discuss how to care for books in order to keep them readable for a long time. Ask the children if they take care of all of their toys. If you have one, show them an old, tattered book and let them see how hard it is to enjoy reading it in that condition.

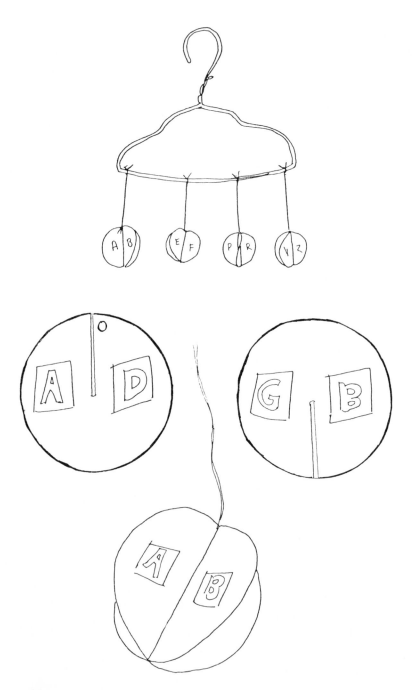

Alphabet or Number Mobile

Materials: coat hangers
colored yarn
heavy paper

Ahead of time: Cut four-inch-diameter circles from colored paper; eight for each child. Cut a slit in each circle half way through to the circle's center. On small squares of paper, write letters or numerals. Cut twelve-inch lengths of yarn.

Kids Do: Each puts his circles together in pairs by slipping slits together as shown. He then pastes letters or numerals on the circles and hangs them from a coat hanger with brightly colored yarn. Children can spin the circles around, or turn them slowly to examine each letter or numeral.

Paper-Plate Clock

Materials: paper plates
paper
lightweight cardboard
paper fasteners

Ahead of time: Cut hands for the clocks from cardboard, as shown. Punch holes in the rounded ends for paper fasteners. Punch holes in the centers of the paper plates. Write numerals on small squares of paper. Mark dots with a crayon on the plates where the numbers will be pasted.

Kids Do: Each colors his plate with crayons or markers and pastes the numbers in the correct places over the marked dots.

The numerals can be handed out one by one so there is no confusion. Center the holes in the hands over the hole in each plate and fasten with the paper fastener. Although the children probably won't be able to tell time for awhile, they can learn to recognize the numbers. If they're going to get a snack at 10:30, set the hands of the paper clock at that position. When the real clock's hands get to the same position, the children will know it's snack time.

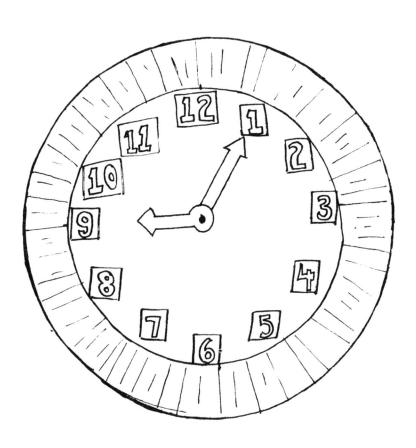

Quill Pen

Materials: ballpoint pens
　　　　colored paper

Ahead of time: Cut rectangles of paper long enough and wide
　　　　enough to encircle the pens. Cut right-angle triangles for
　　　　the quills. The long sides of the triangles should be as long
　　　　as the pens.

Kids Do: Each feathers the edges of his triangle with scissors.
He then tapes the rectangle around the pen to cover it and
tapes the triangle to the pen as shown, leaving enough room to
hold the pen. Let the children practice holding their pens properly as they trace around alphabet stencils or other shapes.

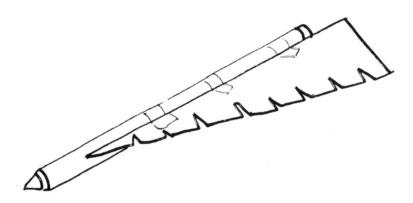

Activities

Letter Bags. Divide the children into two groups, and give each group a grocery bag with a large letter printed on it. You could, for example, use the letters *S* and *B.* Place items whose names begin with those letters in your living room where they can easily be seen by the youngsters. These items could include shoes, spoons, soap, socks, scissors, string, sponges, books, balls, brushes, beanbags, bottles, and buttons. Let the children in each group see how many of the items they can associate with "their" letter, and have them place them in their bag.

Name Recognition. Print each child's first name in large letters and cut the letters out. Pass out all the letters for one child's name and encourage the children to work together to arrange the letters correctly. After they have placed the letters in the proper order, give them the letters for another child's name.

Mixing Colors. Place small jars half full of water on a table, along with red, yellow, and blue food coloring. Let the children put drops of the colors into the jars. What happens when they add yellow to red? Blue to yellow?

Following Directions. Fold a bedsheet in half, and place it on the floor. Have the children stand around the edges of the sheet and follow simple instructions. Ask them, for example, to stand with one foot on the sheet and the other foot off, to take three steps backward from the edge of the sheet, to sit down on the sheet, to lie down with only their heads on the sheet.

Recall Game. Have the children sit on a sofa with a large cardboard box in front of them, with the opening facing away from them. Bring a tray of familiar items to the children and let them examine and identify them for a few minutes. The tray might include a comb, a spoon, a crayon, a book, a toothbrush, a screw driver, a rubber band, a mitten, a toy car, a washcloth, a pair of scissors, and a roll of tape. After the youngsters have identified all of the items, slide the tray inside the box, and ask them to recall as many of the items as they can. Every time an item is recalled, take it out and let the child hold it. If any items remain, give the children hints and let them guess.

Experimenting with Shapes and Sizes. Fill a tumbler half full of dried beans. Then pour them into a shallow dish. Does it look like the same amount? Explain to the children how the same amount of beans can take various shapes. This experiment can be repeated with colored water and other materials in an assortment of containers.

"What Am I" Game. Have the children sit on the floor in a circle. The leader, who is in the center, acts out or describes an animal, plant, or household item. The leader might say, "I am round. I am red. I grow on trees. People like to eat me." By the second or third clue, and certainly by the fourth, the children will have identified what the leader is pretending to be. After this has been done a few times, the youngsters will catch on and should be encouraged to take turns as leader. A shy child may not want to be the leader, but he usually enjoys guessing at what the others are acting out.

"Feeling" the Alphabet. Drawing letters with pencil or crayon is difficult for preschoolers, but they might enjoy tracing letters in wet sand, or forming them with lengths of rope. Letters can also be cut from pieces of sandpaper, and the children can trace over them with their fingers. Some three-year-olds are more interested in working with letters than others. These differences should be respected; no child should be pressured to learn his alphabet in preschool.

Treasure Hunt. Trace the shapes of common household objects on squares of lightweight cardboard with a marking pen. Spread the cards on the floor and place the objects throughout the room. Ask the children to take turns going on a treasure hunt to find objects that fit the shapes on the cards.

Calendar Games. Old calendars can be used in several ways. Children can copy numbers into appropriate squares or just cut out numbers to paste on other paper. If the calendars are large enough, the children can paste the appropriate number of stars in each square. The youngsters can also play "calendar drop" by laying a calendar page on the floor and, while standing straight above it, dropping a button onto it. If it lands on 4, the prize is four raisins, and if it lands on 18 or a higher number, the child gets a whole handful. If the button drops on a low number, let the child have an extra turn. The children will not only learn to count and develop their coordination skills, but they will also enjoy the little snack.

Field Trips. If arrangements are made ahead of time, a special tour of the local library is often possible. The youngsters might be able to view a short cartoon that is in the library files or to listen to a record. The children can browse through picture books and perhaps check some out.

The principal of a local elementary school might be interested in arranging a short tour. While sitting in on a class might not be practical, touring the halls and looking at the gymnasium and cafeteria could be an enlightening experience for the children.

Songs, Rhymes, and Fingerplay

Big A, Little a

Big *A*, little *a*
Bouncing *B*,
The Cat's in the Cupboard
And can't *C* me.

Five Little Monkeys

Five little monkeys went to the store;
One got lost, and then there were four.

Four little monkeys swinging in a tree;
One fell down, and then there were three.

Three little monkeys ate turtle stew;
One got sick, and then there were two.

Two little monkeys lying in the sun;
One shriveled up, and then there was one.

One little monkey couldn't have fun;
He ran away from home, and then there were none.

A Diller, A Dollar

A Diller, a dollar,
A ten o'clock scholar,
What makes you come so soon?
You used to come at ten o'clock
And now you come at noon.

One, Two, Buckle My Shoe

One, two, buckle my shoe,
Three, four, shut the door,
Five, six, pick up sticks,
Seven, eight, lay them straight,
Nine, ten, the big fat hen.

Blue is the Color of the Summer Sky

Blue is the color of the summer sky;
Green is the color of the trees so high;
Yellow is the color of the great big sun;
Red is the apple, please give me one.

A Great Big Ball

A great big ball for Daddy,   [Make large circle with arms.]
A middle-sized ball for
   Mommy,

                                      [Make circle with thumbs and
                                      fore fingers.]
A little ball for me.   [Make circle with one thumb
                                      and fore finger.]

Let's all count together:
   one, two, three.   [Make each as you count
                                      them.]

This Old Man

1. This old man, he played one, he played nick-nack

on my drum.* Nick-nack paddy whack,

give the dog a bone. This old man came rolling home.

*

2) shoe   5) hive   8) gate

3) knee   6) sticks   9) spine

4) door   7) up in   10) hen
              heaven

Hickory, Dickory, Dock

Hickory, dickory, dock! The

mouse ran up the clock. The clock struck one, the

mouse ran down. Hickory, dickory, dock.

Storybook Ideas

Curious George Learns the Alphabet, H. A. Rey (Houghton Mifflin, 1963).

Alligators All Around—An Alphabet, Maurice Sendak (Harper and Row, 1962).

Ten What? A Mystery Counting Book, Russell Hoban and Sylvie Selig (Scribner's, 1974).

The Adventures of the Three Colors, Annette Tison and Talus Taylor (World, 1971).

Chicken Little, Count-to-Ten, Margaret Friskey and Katherine Evans (Childrens Press, 1946).

One Monday Morning, Uri Shulevitz (Scribner's, 1967).

Apricot ABC, Miska Miles (Little, Brown, 1969).

Colors, John J. Reiss (Bradbury Press, 1974).

Sixes and Sevens, John Yeoman and Quentin Blake (Macmillan, 1971).

Ten Bears in My Bed: A Goodnight Countdown, Stan Mack (Pantheon, 1974).

Inside, Outside, Upside Down, Stan and Jan Berenstain (Random House, 1968).

Fun With ABC and 1-2-3, Hal Dareff (Parents' Magazine Press, 1965).

Two Lonely Ducks: A Counting Book, Roger Duvoisin (Knopf, 1955).

13

Discovering Our Faith

All of the Discovery chapters in this book can be easily adapted to a religious theme. A church-centered school has myriad opportunities to teach children about God. Paperwork can be captioned "Thank God for our pets," or "God made the flowers," or "God loves everyone." Crafts can be God-centered and special prayers can be learned for those holidays that have religious significance. When you discuss family life, tell about Jacob and Esau, Mary and Martha, and Joseph and his brothers. If you are talking about different occupations in the Bible, talk about carpenters, shepherds, and priests. Tell the children that teachers, policemen, and storekeepers can still be God's helpers in different ways. The Garden of Eden is a perfect setting for a discussion of God's creations in the environment. Biblical animals also make interesting stories: Daniel in the lion's den, Noah's ark, Jonah and the whale, and Jesus riding a donkey are fascinating to little ones. Most bookstores have Children's Bibles, which can supplement story time.

Paper Work

Open the Church Doors. Cut church shapes from a sheet of white or light-colored construction paper. Draw arched windows and double doors that meet at the center. Cut the doors and fold them back to open and close. Cut pointed strips of paper for steeples. Let each child paste a church and steeple on a sheet of backing paper, making sure that the doors are not pasted shut. The children can paste catalog cutouts of people inside the church doors and cut bits of colored paper to paste onto windows for a stained-glass look. Talk about the importance of going to church and learning about God.

Table Prayer. Draw outlines of cereal bowls on heavy paper using a felt marker. On separate pieces of paper letter, GOD IS GREAT, GOD IS GOOD, LET US THANK HIM FOR OUR FOOD. Have each child paste the prayer next to a bowl outline. The children can glue bits of dry cereal inside the bowl outline. Teach them the prayer, and encourage them to say it before snacks and meals.

Draw a Cross. Make outlines of crosses with unconnected short lines. Let the children fill in the spaces between the lines to complete their crosses, and then color or paint them for a finished look.

Creation Cube. Use a cube-shaped box (somewhat smaller than a shoebox) for each child and tape the top shut. Cut pictures from calendars and magazines that represent each of the six days of creation: (1) day and night, (2) land and water, (3) vegetation, (4) sun, moon, and stars, (5) fish and fowl, (6) animals and man. Let the children paste pictures on each of the six sides of their cubes. The number representing the day can be written or pasted on each picture.

"Thank You, Lord," Poster. Cut from magazines pictures of such things as people, animals, flowers, houses, toys, and food. Letter THANK YOU, LORD, on the top of a large sheet of paper and let each child choose things for which he is especially thankful to paste on his poster. Talk about the many things we have God to thank for, and encourage each child to say his own prayer of thanks to Him.

God Loves Us. Before your session, cut strips two inches wide from the length of a piece of construction paper. On separate pieces of paper, letter GOD LOVES in one-inch lettering, leaving at least three inches at the right side of the paper. To the right of "God Loves," make two horizontal slits, one above the other and one inch apart, wide enough for the two-inch strip to fit through. Write the name of each child on the strips, one above the other and at least one inch apart. Thread the strip through the two slits from the back. Children will enjoy pulling the strip up and down as they read "God Loves" with their own name and the names of their friends.

Crafts

Scroll

Materials: typing paper
    twelve-inch dowel sticks
    magazines
    yarn

Ahead of time: Letter GOD IS LOVE on small pieces of paper.

Kids Do: The children look through magazines and find pictures representing love, such as a mother with her baby or a

child with his pet. Help the children cut their pictures out and paste them on the typing paper along with "God Is Love." Glue the sticks to the tops and bottoms of the papers. Help the children roll the papers into scrolls. Tell them what the message on their scrolls says. Talk about how God loves them and cares for them all the time. Use pieces of yarn to tie the scrolls.

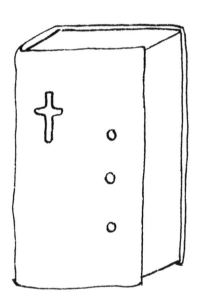

Soap Bible

Materials: face-sized bars of soap
    white felt
    wide gold ribbon
    foil
    sequins

Ahead of time: Cut pieces of felt to fit around the bars of soap, and cut the ribbon so that it will fit around three of the outer edges of the bars, as illustrated. Cut the foil into small crosses.

Kids Do: Each glues a ribbon around three outer edges of a soap bar to represent the edges of the pages and glues a felt "book jacket" around the front, spine, and back of the "Bible." A cross and some sequins are added for more decoration.

Noah's Ark

Materials: shoe boxes
     margarine tubs
     magazines

Ahead of time: Cut pictures of animals from magazines or trace them on colored paper.

Kids Do: They paint their boxes brown or cover them with brown paper and paste animal pictures on the sides. Turn the margarine tubs upside down and glue them to the boxes, as shown. Describe an ark to the children and tell the Bible story of Noah. Ask the children to name all the animals they can. What would the world be like without all the animals?

Angel

Materials: heavy white paper
    pipe cleaners
    gummed stars
    small Christmas balls, ping-pong balls, or styrofoam balls

Ahead of time: Cut half circles eight inches in diameter from
    white paper. Form cones, and staple. Cut one-half inch
    from the top of each cone to make an opening for a ball to
    rest on. Cut wing shapes as shown.

Kids Do: Each tapes a ball on top of a cone, puts gummed stars in place, and tapes wings behind the cone. The pipe cleaners can be formed into halos and taped onto the backs of the angels' heads. Talk about guardian angels and angels in the Bible who were sent from heaven to praise God.

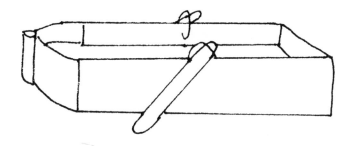

Peter's Fishing Boat

Materials: milk cartons
      popsicle sticks
      paper clips

Ahead of time: Cut the milk cartons in half as shown.

Kids Do: Each attaches paper clips to his boat for oarlocks and slips popsicle sticks into them for oars. The children can sail their boats in the bath tub—their make-believe Sea of Galilee. Fish shapes that will float can be cut from carton scraps, and the children can catch them with small pieces of nylon netting or nylon stocking.

Cross Necklace

Materials: ice cream sticks
      yarn

Ahead of time: Break half of the sticks in two equal pieces and smooth the broken edges with sandpaper. Punch holes in one end of each whole stick.

Kids Do: Each colors a whole stick and a half stick with a felt marker or bright paint. When they are dry, he glues them together in the form of a cross. "God Loves Me" can be written with a marking pen, as shown. Wrap short lengths of yarn in front of the horizontal sticks and behind the vertical ones, and tie in back. Pass longer pieces of yarn through the holes at the top of the crosses so they can be worn around the neck. Tell the children that if anyone asks what it means, they can say, "Jesus died on the cross because He loves us."

Activities

Bible Story Flash Cards. Collect pictures from Sunday school papers depicting simple Bible stories. Glue the pictures onto lightweight cardboard to make a set of Bible flash cards. Once the children become familiar with the stories, let each one choose a card to explain to the rest of the group.

The Lost Coin. The New Testament stories of the lost coin and the lost sheep can be turned into games that are fun for little children, while at the same time bringing life into Biblical truths. Hide a coin or a toy lamb in a place where a child would be able to find it. Tell the children the Bible story (Luke 15), and then let them search for what is "lost."

Light Under a Bushel. A simple procedure can give new meaning to "This Little Light of Mine" (page 219): Light a short candle and place it under a "bushel" (tin can). Not only will the light be hidden, as the song says, but without air, the flame will soon go out. Talk about what it means for a person to let his light shine for the Lord.

Bible Drama. Help the children act out simple Bible stories such as the Good Samaritan, the Ten Lepers, and Daniel in the Lion's Den.

Bible Clothes. Sandals: Cut child-sized foot shapes from carpet scraps, upholstery vinyl, or heavy cardboard. Punch three holes in each side. The children can lace long pieces of cord through holes, over the foot, and around the ankle, as shown. Tie around the calf. *Robe:* Cut two-by-four-foot pieces from old sheets or bedspreads and cut holes in the centers large enough for the childrens' heads. Use scraps of material for belts. *Headdress:* Cut scraps of material into two-foot squares, and cut bands of material long enough to fit around the childrens' heads. Tie the scraps around their heads with the bands.

Children can dress up as Bible people and act out almost any Biblical story. They can hold a staff and pretend to be David the shepherd. They can make a tent from a bedspread draped over chairs and sleep on mats in the tent for rest time. They can sample dates and figs for their snack. Let them balance empty bleach bottles on their heads and pretend to carry water for their imaginary camels. Talk to them about children's lives in Bible times, and how God loves all children.

Field Trips. Make arrangements with a local minister to have a tour of a church. If possible, let the children experience what it is like to sit in the choir loft and to stand behind the pulpit. Let them feel the shiny choir robes and look into the minister's study. Talk to the minister about serving the Lord. How can little children be God's helpers?

Prayers, Poems, and Songs

God Is Great

God is Great;
God is Good.
Let us thank Him
For our food.   Amen.

Come, Lord Jesus

Come, Lord Jesus, be our guest;
Let this food to us be blest.
Our hands we fold, our heads we bow.
For food and drink, we thank thee now.   Amen.

Thank You, Lord, for Sunshine

Thank you, Lord, for sunshine
And for the sky above,
But most of all I thank you
For your gentle love.   Amen.

Sharing

Sharing all my games and toys,
With other little girls and boys,
Is how God would have me be,
For He shared His love with me.

God Cares for Little Children

God cares for little children,
In a very special way.
He's with them when they eat and sleep,
And when they work and play.

This Is the Church

This is the church,   [Interlace fingers with
                              knuckles showing upwards.]

This is the steeple;   [Point index fingers up to
                              make a steeple.]

Open the doors,   [Bring thumbs outward to
                              "open doors."]

And see all the people.   [Open hands to expose fingers.]

This Little Light

1. This little light of mine, I'm gonna let it

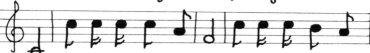

shine. This little light of mine, I'm gonna let it

shine, let it shine, let it shine, let it shine.

2. Don't let Satan (blow) it out, I'm gonna let it shine. (Repeat)
   Let it shine, let it shine, let it shine.

3. Hide it under a bushel? No! I'm gonna let it shine. (Repeat)
   Let it shine, let it shine, let it shine.

4. Let it shine till Jesus comes, I'm gonna let it shine. (Repeat)
   Let it shine, let it shine, let it shine.

God is so Good

God is so good, God is so good;

God is so good, He's so good to me.

God answers prayer, God answers prayer;
God answers prayer, He's so good to me.

God sent his son, God sent his son;
God sent his son, He's so good to me.

Oh, Be Careful

1. Oh, be careful little mouth what you

say; Oh, be careful little mouth what you say; For the

Father up above is looking down in love, so be

careful little mouth what you say.

2. Oh, be careful little ears what you hear...
3. Oh, be careful little eyes what you see...
4. Oh, be careful little hands what you do...
5. Oh, be careful little feet where you walk...

221

Storybook Ideas

A Basket in the Reeds, Raphael Saporta (Lerner Publications, 1965).

To Church We Go, Robbie Trent (Follett, 1956).

Jesus, the Little New Baby, Mary E. Lloyd (Abingdon-Cokesbury Press, 1951).

Noah and the Great Flood, Warwick Hutton (Atheneum, 1977).

David and the Giant, Mike McClenlock (Harper and Brothers, 1960).

Jonah and the Great Fish, Clyde R. Bulla (Crowell, 1970).

Noah and the Rainbow, Max Bollinger (Crowell, 1972).

The First Seven Days, illustrated by Paul Galdone (Crowell, 1962).

A Donkey For the King, John and Patricia Beatty (Macmillan, 1966).

Small Rain: Verses From the Bible, Jessie O. Jones (Viking, 1949).

Why Noah Chose the Dove, Isaac B. Singer (Farrar, Straus and Giroux, 1973).

Prayer For a Child, Rachel Field (Macmillan, 1941).

In the Beginning, Alf Evers (Macmillan, 1954).

14

Discovering Exercises
and Games

Exercises and games add to the health and happiness of preschoolers. A strong, agile body enables a youngster to play and
learn more efficiently. Of course, preschoolers are not adults
and should not be expected to do exercises that adults enjoy;
jumping jacks, sit-ups, and the like are too advanced for most
three-year-olds. However, there are many simple coordination
and body-building activities that they can perform easily and
enjoy doing. Often, children enjoy creating their own frolic-
some actions; "snake stomping" and "fly swatting" were favorites in our group. Above all, exercise time should be fun; the
children should look forward to it. Even a reluctant child will
soon join in of his own accord if the others are having fun.

Hand and Finger Exercises

The tiny muscles in children's hands need practice in coordination. Fortunately, many play activities provide this practice
naturally. Working with puzzles, tearing paper, stringing
beads, and any painting, coloring, mixing, or stirring activities
require children to use their small muscles. Fingerpainting
and sand painting are ideal. Painting with eyedroppers and
hanging objects with clip clothespins encourage them to
squeeze. Rolling, patting, pounding, and shaping clay with
cookie cutters helps to develop finger coordination, as does shoe

lacing, buttoning, and snapping. A peg board can be set up and the children can place golf tees in the holes to make different designs. When a design is created, a long length of yarn can be tied around one of the tees and the children shown how to wrap it around different tees, stringing it from tee to tee to create a colorful pattern.

Set up coin races, rice races, dried pea races, or even raisin races, if you don't mind a little nibbling. Pour some rice on the table and ask the children to pick it up as quickly as they can and put it into baby food jars, or cut a slit in the top of a margarine tub and have the children drop coins through the slot.

Finger coordination can be developed through paper-folding activities. Ask the children to fold and crease paper into different shapes and practice stuffing it into envelopes.

Finger plays and hand plays are always favorites. Ask the children to make their index and middle fingers "walk" around furniture and toys. Have them count on their fingers, holding up two or three fingers while keeping the others curled. They may also enjoy trying to snap their fingers. Teach the children to act out a rhyme that requires them to use their hands in many different positions. For example:

> Open, shut them; open, shut them;
> Give a little clap.
> Open, shut them; open, shut them;
> Lay them in your lap.
>
> Creep them, creep them, creep them, creep them,
> Way up to your chin.
> Open up your little mouth,
> But do not let them in.
>
> Open, shut them; open, shut them,
> To your shoulders fly.
> Then like little birdies,
> Flutter to the sky.
>
> Falling, falling, falling, falling,
> Almost to the ground.

Quickly pick them up again,
And turn them round and round.
Faster, faster, faster, faster,
Slower, slower, slower, slower,
Clap!

Eye-Hand Coordination

Games of throwing, catching, and aiming at targets help improve coordination between the eye and the hand. Tossing beanbags at targets is a game with infinite variations. Cut a hole in a large box and decorate it as a clown with an open mouth for a target. Children can toss the beanbags from lying, sitting, and standing positions and from various distances. Try having one child catch a beanbag in a salad bowl when the bag is tossed by his partner. Use old bleach or detergent bottles for bowling pins, and let the children try to knock them over with beanbags or tennis balls. Bottles of this type can also be used for ring toss games. Rings can be made from lengths of clothesline stiffened by wire pushed through the centers and entwined to form a circle.

Another target game involves dropping clothespins into jars. Have the children kneel on a heavy, sturdy chair, resting their arms on the back to aim and drop. The children can also learn eye-hand coordination by standing in a circle and throwing a ball into a clothes basket in the center; each time a child is successful, he moves one step backward. Badminton birdies, ping pong balls, or even wads of paper can replace more conventional balls. Children also enjoy a pint-sized version of basketball. Make a hoop out of a coat hanger and hang it on a door knob. Balloons or wads of paper can be used instead of balls.

Catching or hitting small balls is difficult for preschoolers. Start with a large beach ball and have the children catch it from sitting, kneeling, or standing positions. Ask each child to bend at the hips with his legs spread apart and catch a ball rolled from behind him. Have the youngsters use a yardstick to hit a balloon or beach ball suspended from the ceiling. "Baseball" can be played with a broom and a beach ball, and "volleyball" can be played by patting balloons back and forth.

Balancing Activities

Exercises that improve a child's balance can be done with or without props. Encourage the children to try balancing on one foot. Ask them to close their eyes or bend down and pick something off the floor while doing so. Place two lengths of rope six or eight inches apart, parallel to each other, and ask the children to walk between them. Then prop a two-by-four on low boxes and ask the youngsters to walk the length of the board by stepping sideways. When they have mastered this, they can try walking forward while keeping one foot ahead of the other all the way across. Then they can try to alternate feet, spreading their arms for balance.

When old magazines are scattered around a room, the children can pretend to "cross a river" by stepping from one to the other without "getting their feet wet." Walking across a room with objects balanced on their heads, in their hands, in baskets, or on spoons held in front of them are all good exercises in balance, as is passing marbles back and forth to each other on spoons.

Obstacle Course

An obstacle course improves large muscle control and gives practice in following directions. It can be simple or elaborate, and can be set up outdoors or indoors. At first, the children "follow the leader" through the course; then they follow verbal instructions; finally, they try to remember the course entirely on their own. They can crawl *under* chairs, rope, yardsticks, tables, wagons, or bushes. They can run, walk, crawl, hop, or go on tiptoe *around* almost anything. They can step *between* rungs of ladders lying on the ground or floor, or between lines made of chalk or rope. They can climb *up and down* stairs made from wooden boxes of varied sizes. They can jump, crawl, or step *over* blocks, pillows, wastebaskets, or cardboard boxes. They can try going *in and out* of a large cardboard box with a sliding cardboard door on one end. Going *through* tires, cardboard boxes with the bottoms and tops cut out, or hoops is fun; long tunnels are even more so. One can be made by covering two rows of chairs with a blanket or by tying several inner-tubes together. Several large boxes of different sizes with the ends cut out can make a long tunnel with varying heights.

Your obstacle course should not be a test of speed. Preschoolers will be doing well if they don't knock anything over.

Stretching and Curling

When doing exercises involving the entire body, avoid hard, fast, jerky movements, which tighten muscles. Concentrate on smooth, fluid motion. Stretching and curling exercises are very effective when done in slow motion.

Have the children sit on the floor, grasp their knees, and bring them to their chests; then ask them to roll backward slowly without letting go of their knees. Have the youngsters pretend to be sprouting tulips by squatting with their hands close to their feet; keeping hands and feet "planted" on the floor, they raise their hips and try to straighten their legs without "uprooting" themselves. Children also enjoy playing "seesaw." Two of them sit on the floor facing each other with their legs straight out and the soles of their shoes touching. They lean forward, clasp each others' hands, and rock gently forward and backward imitating a seesaw (1). Other stretching exercises include standing on tiptoes and reaching as high as possible, and touching the floor without bending the knees. Youngsters also enjoy lying on their stomachs on the floor and trying to touch their heads with their toes by raising their heads backwards and bending their knees.

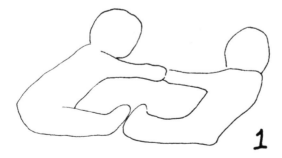

1

Coordination and Muscle Building

There are many exercises designed to help build strength, coordination, and posture control. These involve using the larger muscles of the legs, arms, and back and moving the whole body as a unit. The "animal-pretending" activities in chapter eight are excellent for this purpose.

"Angels" is also a game which children enjoy. Lying on their backs on the floor, legs together and hands at their sides, they raise their hands, arms straight, to touch above their heads; at the same time, they spread their straightened legs as far apart as possible. They then return to the original position. If they cannot do this successfully, have them try one limb at a time, or arms first and then legs.

There are a number of ways to help develop arm and upper-body muscles. One of these is playing "Wheelbarrow." One child walks on his hands while his partner walks behind him holding his ankles. A pull-up bar is also helpful. You can easily construct one in a doorway. Cut notches large enough to hold a heavy-duty broomstick in blocks of wood, and fasten these wooden brackets into a door jamb with heavy-duty wood screws. Place them at varying heights so the bar can be adjusted to the level of each child's chest (2). Each child should hold the bar and slide his feet underneath it, keeping his body and arms straight (2). Then he should pull himself up slowly so that his chest touches the bar and his body remains straight. After holding this position for a few moments, he can let himself down slowly and repeat the process. The bar can also be used to teach children to hang by their knees.

The children can easily exercise their legs while lying on their backs on the floor. Have them pretend to ride bicycles to grandma's house by making pumping motions with their legs while keeping their hips on the floor. They can also pretend, while lying on their backs, to be different types of tools: scissors (spreading their legs in the air and crossing them over each other and back again), hammers (holding a leg straight upward and striking it repeatedly with the other leg), staplers (spreading legs apart and quickly snapping them together and back), sewing machines (keeping both legs together and imitating the movement of a wheel).

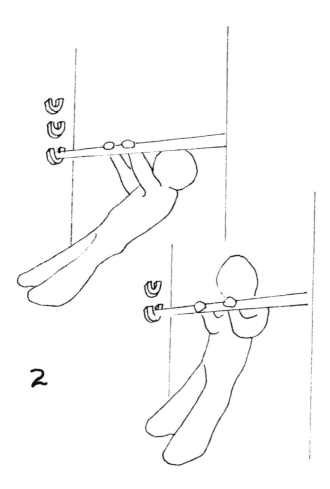

2

Jumping

Jumping exercises can build leg strength and body coordination. Let the children jump from one level to another. Choose a stair step or some other firm surface. The youngsters can jump down from the step using both feet to take off and both to land. Or they can take off using one foot and land on two. For more of a challenge they can take off using one foot and land on one foot. Then they can try to jump up to a raised surface; if they can do this using both feet, have them try with one.

Jumping on level surfaces can also be challenging. Ask the children to run and jump forward using one foot to take off and one or both to land. Have them stand behind a yardstick or length of rope lying on the floor and jump as far forward as they can. A target distance could be set with another rope or yardstick. The youngsters can also practice their skills by hopping, skipping, and side-skipping. On a nice day, take them outside and draw a hopscotch layout on the sidewalk. They won't understand the rules of the game, but they'll enjoy jumping through the squares on one and both feet.

"Jack be nimble, Jack be quick, Jack jump over the candlestick," is an ideal nursery rhyme for practicing jumps over objects. The children may fall, so use pillows, stuffed animals, or paper cones as "candlesticks." They may also want to try jumping backwards over the objects, or jumping over them on one foot.

Exercises to Music

Children enjoy doing exercises to music. They can run on their toes, walk tiptoe, run and hop, and gallop and trot to varying speeds of music. Clapping while they do these movements requires a bit more coordination. Ask them to run while the music plays, and to stop quickly when the music stops. They can whirl by themselves or holding hands with a partner. Since preschoolers tend to get carried away, be sure to follow fast movements with slower ones.

Children enjoy clapping in rhythm, and a marching band with homemade instruments is certain to capture their interest. Three simple instruments you can make with your group are the tambourine, tom-tom, and trumpet. Tambourine: Staple two paper plates together, leaving a small opening to insert dried peas or beans. Let each child decorate his instrument, pour in the beans, and seal the opening (A). Tom-tom: Let the youngsters decorate salt or oatmeal boxes and fill them with

230

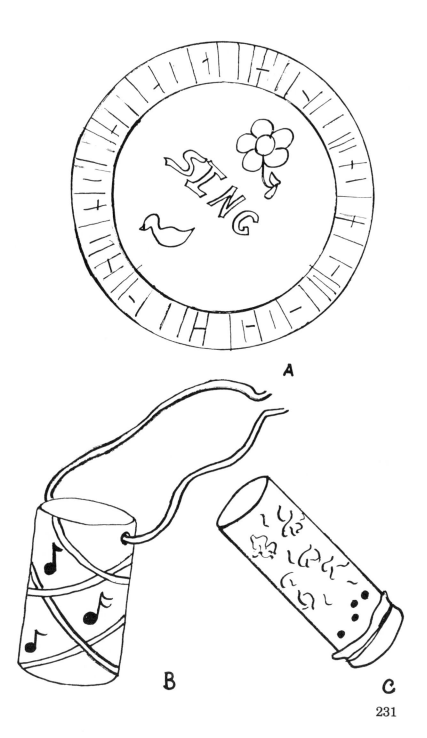

A

B

C

dried beans. Attach string or lightweight cord so the children can hang the drums around their necks and beat them with their hands (B). Trumpet: Attach waxed paper to one end of a paper-towel tube with a rubber band. Punch a few holes in the tube. After each child has decorated his trumpet, he can hum into it (C).

Games

Action games provide an enjoyable way for youngsters to exercise together. Preschoolers often like to play games even when they don't understand all the rules. Many games of "Hide and Seek" turn into giggling sessions when hiding places are revealed too early because youngsters can't wait to be "found."

Tag can be played in an organized fashion by using variations such as "Duck, Duck, Goose" or "Drop the Handkerchief." In "Duck, Duck, Goose" the children squat down in a circle and one is chosen to be "it." He walks around tapping each of the others on the head as he says "duck" or "goose." If he calls "duck," the tapped child remains squatting, but if he calls "goose," the child must get up and chase him around the circle to the original position. If he makes it without getting tagged, the other child becomes "it" and the process begins again. "Drop the Handkerchief" is similar, except that the children stand and the child who is "it" drops a handkerchief or a piece of cloth at their feet. "Freeze Tag" is an enjoyable outdoor game; when the chaser tags a child, the child must try to hold his position, and if he can't, he becomes "it."

Mimicking the movements of others is a good way to practice following directions. While three- and four-year-olds may be a bit young to play "Simon Says," "Follow the Leader" is just right for them. The children can imitate the leader who touches his nose to his knees, holds his toes with his hands, stretches his hands high in the air, touches his right ear with his left hand, holds his left ankle with his right hand, and so on. This teaches little ones to follow instructions and improves body awareness.

"Ring Around the Rosy" is a fun game for little children and it can be played with many variations. As they hold hands in a circle, the children sing:

> Ring around the rosy,
> A pocket full of posies,
> Ashes, ashes, (1) we all fall down.
>   (2) we all jump up.
>   (3) we all kneel down.
>   (4) we all bow down.
>   (5) we all hop around.
>   (6) we all turn around.
>   (7) we all sit still.

"Musical Chairs" is a game that is simple to understand and is one that children enjoy playing. Place a row of chairs in the middle of the room so they face forward and backward alternately. Use one less chair than the number of children in the group. The youngsters march around the chairs to music, and when the music stops, they scramble to sit on the chairs. The child who doesn't get a chair is "out." One chair is then removed, and this routine is repeated until there is only one chair left for two children. Whoever gets this chair when the music stops is the winner.

"London Bridge" can be played with as few as three or four children. Two players form an arch by holding their hands above their heads as the others march around them and pass under the bridge. Everyone sings:

> London Bridge is falling down,
> Falling down, falling down;
> London Bridge is falling down,
> My fair lady (gentleman).

As they sing "My fair lady," the bridge encircles the child who is underneath at the time and swings him back and forth while singing:

> Take the keys and lock her up,
> Lock her up, lock her up;
> Take the keys and lock her up,
> My fair lady.

Guessing games make ideal quiet indoor activities. In "Blind Man's Bluff" a blindfolded child walks around among the other children and tries to guess who they are by feeling their hair, clothes, and facial features. When the child guesses correctly, the identified child has a try. In "Button, Button," all but two of the youngsters can sit side by side on a sofa with their hands cupped on their laps. The child who is leader pretends to drop a button into each child's hands, and then all the children close their "cups," although only one has been given the button. The other child calls "Button, button, who's got the button?" as he tries to guess who has it. If he guesses correctly, he changes places with the child who had the button, and the game repeats itself.

Appendix One

Recipes for Arts, Crafts and Simple Foods

One of the best ways to keep expenses low in your home nursery school is to construct most of the crafts from throw-away scraps and used household items. In addition, paints, paste, clay, and plasters can be homemade. The following recipes tell how to make materials for the crafts described above. These can be made in large quantities and stored for future use.

We have also included simple cookie and treat recipes that the children can help make.

Paints and Paste

Soapsuds Paint

1 cup soap flakes
4 tablespoons water
$^1/_2$ teaspoon tempera paint

Mix soap flakes and water together. Beat with an eggbeater until mixture reaches the consistency of whipped cream. Add tempera paint.

Jiffy Fingerpaint

$^1/_2$ cup flour
2 cups water
1 tablespoon glycerine
food coloring

Mix flour with a small amount of water to form a thick paste. Add the remainder of the water. Cook over a low heat and stir constantly until mixture is thick and clear. When cool, add glycerine. Separate mixture into small containers and add desired food coloring.

Cornstarch Paint

3 tablespoons cornstarch
2 cups water
1 tablespoon glycerine
food coloring or tempera paint

Mix cornstarch with a small amount of water. Stir vigorously to form a smooth paste. Add the remainder of the water. Cook over a low heat and stir constantly until mixture begins to boil. When cool, add glycerine. Add food coloring or tempera paint.

Sand Painting

$1/2$ cup sand (washed, dried, and sifted)
$1/2$ teaspoon powdered paint
6 tablespoons white household glue
3 tablespoons warm water

Mix sand and powder paint together. Set aside. Mix water and glue together and spread it over a design on a heavy sheet of paper or cardboard. Sprinkle sand mixture over glue-coated paper and allow to dry.

Flour Paste

$1/2$ cup flour
2 tablespoons sugar
1 cup warm water
$1/4$ teaspoon oil of wintergreen

Mix flour and sugar together. Add a small amount of water. Stir vigorously to prevent lumps. Add remainder of water and cook over a low heat, stirring constantly. When cool, add oil of wintergreen.

Modeling Compounds

Play-clay

1 cup flour
$^1/_2$ cup salt
2 teaspoons cream of tartar
1 tablespoon vegetable oil
1 cup water
$^1/_2$ teaspoon oil of wintergreen
food coloring

Mix dry ingredients together. Add oil and water. Cook over a slow heat until thick. Store in a covered, airtight container.

Baker's Clay

1 cup salt
$1^1/_2$ cup warm water
4 cups flour

Dissolve salt in warm water. Add flour and mix. Knead five minutes. Mold desired forms from pieces of dough, or cut shapes from rolled out clay with floured cookie cutters. Place on greased cookie sheet and bake at 275° for one hour.

Soap Powder Clay

$1^1/_2$ cups soap powder
2 tablespoons warm water

Mix soap powder and water in mixing bowl. Beat with an electric mixer until mixture is thick and claylike. Mold into desired figures and forms. The clay dries to a hard finish.

Papier-Mâché

$^1/_2$ cup flour
$^1/_4$ cup powdered resin glue
1 pint water
newspapers

Mix flour, glue, and water together in a large bowl or pan. Tear newspapers into small pieces and strips and soak in mixture until soft. Attach to desired form and allow several hours for drying.

Alternative Recipe: Tear up newspapers into small pieces. Soak in warm water until soft. Mix with small amount of laundry starch that has been cooked until creamy.

Crepe-Paper Modeling Compound

2 cups shredded crepe paper
2 cups water
1 cup flour
2 teaspoons salt

Soak shredded crepe paper in water for several hours until soft. Pour off excess water. Add flour and salt mixture and stir until stiff. Add more flour if necessary. Mold into desired shapes and figures. Dries to a hard finish.

Sawdust Clay

2 cups fine sawdust
$^1/_2$ cup flour
2 tablespoons sugar
1 cup water
$^1/_4$ teaspoon oil of wintergreen (optional)

Make paste mixture by mixing flour, sugar and water. Cook over a slow heat, stirring constantly. Remove from heat and add oil of wintergreen. Mix with sawdust and knead. Add food coloring if desired. Model desired forms as with clay. Allow two or three days to dry, or bake at 200° for one and a half hours.

Sand Plaster

2 cups sand (washed, dried, and sifted)
1 cup cornstarch
2 teaspoons powdered alum
$1^1/_2$ cups hot water

Mix sand, cornstarch, and alum together. Add water and stir until well mixed. Cook over a medium heat, stirring constantly, until thick. Mold into sculptures as desired, and allow to dry in the sun for three or four days.

Cookies and Treats

Quick Chocolate Chip Cookies

1 box yellow cake mix
2 eggs
2 tablespoons water
$^1/_2$ cup vegetable oil
12 oz. package chocolate chips
chopped nuts (optional)

Mix everything together in one bowl. Drop cookies onto a greased cookie sheet. Bake at 375 ° for ten to twelve minutes or until light brown.

Gingerbread Cookies

$^1/_2$ cup margarine
$^1/_2$ cup brown sugar
$^1/_2$ cup molasses
$2^1/_2$ cups flour
$^1/_2$ teaspoon ground ginger
$^1/_2$ teaspoon cinnamon
$^1/_4$ teaspoon salt
$^1/_2$ teaspoon baking soda

Cream margarine and brown sugar together in a large bowl. Add molasses and mix well. Sift dry ingredients together and add to creamy mixture. Stir well and knead. Roll out dough and cut figures of gingerbread men. Bake at 375° for ten to twelve minutes.

Rice Krispy Marshmallow Treats

1/4 cup margarine
1 ten oz. package marshmallows
5 cups Rice Krispies

Melt margarine in large pan on low heat. Add marshmallows and stir until melted. Cook three minutes. Remove from heat and add cereal. Stir until well coated. Using a buttered spatula, press into a buttered cake pan. Allow to cool, and cut into squares.

Granola

2 cups rolled oats
2 tablespoons sesame seeds
1/2 cup coconut
1/4 cup sunflower seeds
3 tablespoons vegetable oil
3 tablespoons honey
1/2 teaspoon salt

Mix everything together. Spread on a cookie sheet. Bake at 450° for about ten minutes, stirring often. When cool, add dates or raisins.

Lollipops

10 ice cream sticks
1/4 cup margarine
1/2 cup light corn syrup
3/4 cup sugar
food coloring

Place ice cream sticks on a lightly buttered baking sheet. Combine ingredients and heat to boiling, stirring occasionally. Reduce heat and continue cooking until a few drops of syrup dropped into very cold water separate into threads which are hard but not brittle. Drop syrup over end of each stick and cool thoroughly before removing from baking sheet.

Yum Yums

Mix milk and powdered sugar to make a thick icing. Add food coloring or cocoa, if desired. Give each child oyster crackers to frost by dipping in the icing.

Chocolate-Graham Bars

Top graham crackers with squares of chocolate, and place in a warm oven until the chocolate is soft and begins to melt. Remove and allow to cool.

Peanut-Buttered Popcorn

Melt two tablespoons of peanut butter and one tablespoon of butter over a very low heat. Pour over a large bowl of popped corn and mix well.

Cheese and Cracker Supreme

Top a soda cracker with a piece of cheese. Decorate with raisins or small pieces of carrot. Place in a warm oven until cheese is soft and begins to melt. Remove and allow to cool.

Nonsticky Travel Snack

Collect some crunchy food items such as popcorn, peanuts, unsweetened breakfast cereals, and pretzels. The children can help you mix the ingredients and put them in small plastic sandwich bags. This treat is ideal for field trips.

Caramel Popcorn Balls

Melt one fourteen-ounce bag of caramels together with two tablespoons of water. Cool slightly, and in a greased bowl, add to sixteen cups of popped corn mixed with one cup of peanuts. Mix thoroughly. After the children have dipped their hands in cold water, they can help shape the mixture into popcorn balls on squares of waxed paper.

Appendix Two

State Regulation and Licensing

Although nursery schools are usually designed to provide pre-school education rather than just two or three hours of day care, most state governments do not distinguish between nursery schools and day-care centers in making their licensing rules. Where nursery schools are regulated, they are generally required to conform to day-care-center standards. This was the policy of the Texas licensing body, for example, until that agency began hearing from nursery schools who "insisted day care center standards were inappropriate to them." The regulations on nap facilities, hot meals, and sick care facilities just were not applicable. In response to these complaints, Texas developed new requirements specifically designed for nursery schools.

However, Texas is an exception. Only a handful of states have formulated regulations specifically for nursery schools. This may be due to the fact that state departments of education rarely regulate nursery schools. Maryland is one of the few states where the state Department of Education assumes direct responsibility for preschool licensing. In Delaware, a voluntary organization of kindergarten and preschool groups makes rules for self-regulation. In New York and Oregon, the state departments of education register some nursery schools on a voluntary basis. In Kentucky, the departments of Education and Human Resources cooperate to regulate nursery schools.

A letter from the Kentucky Department of Human Resources shows a unique awareness of the problem and the need for neighborhood nursery schools: "We certainly do encourage facilities to locate in neighborhoods near the children's homes. The local zoning ordinances often make this impossible." More than a dozen states have no rules at all for nursery schools. In others, agencies not directly connected with education control nursery school operations.

In places where there are no nursery school safety and health standards, children may be physically jeopardized. Problems which arise from inappropriate rules are less obvious; laws which require compliance to unrealistic standards often make nursery schools unavailable where most needed.

What about home nursery schools? Are they regulated by state agencies, and do they require licensing? A home nursery school is exempted from licensing and regulation in most states if it has at least one of the following characteristics:

(1) The teaching mothers receive no pay for their services.
(2) The teaching mothers do not provide care for other children in their homes on a "regular" basis (i.e., the same days for several consecutive weeks).
(3) The teaching mothers have the children in their homes for less than four hours at a time.
(4) There are fewer than four, five, or six children, other than the teaching mother's own child. (See below for your state's requirement.)

Minnesota requires that you care for children for no more than thirty days in any calendar year, and Kentucky requires that the school meets no more than once a week at any one home. A home nursery school could work around such stipulations to avoid the red tape involved in licensing.

Other states add more complications to their requirements. Hawaii, in regulations proposed in March 1978, defined a day-care center as:

A place maintained by any individual, organization or agency for the purpose of providing care for children with or without charging a fee during any part of a twenty-four hour day, regardless of the duration of operation. The term Day Care Center shall include: day nurseries, nursery school groups, preschool, child play groups, parent cooperatives. . . .

In Wisconsin licensing regulations applied to cooperative groups until officials discovered that "difficulties do arise on the issue, and various attempts have been made by some citizens to reconsider." Regulations are currently being revised to allow cooperative groups to exist independently provided that any payments exchanged actually would be used for supplies or equipment.

State agencies should be checked with to be certain what rules may apply. While the previously listed points may release a preschool from licensing obligations, licensing is not necessarily something to be avoided at all costs. It could provide a measure of security and peace of mind to realize that the homes being used for your school pass state inspection. And if questions should arise, it's nice to be "approved."

If your home nursery school requires a license, in almost all cases it will be issued for a family day-care home rather than a nursery school. Those few states that have specific requirements for nursery schools usually license for more than eight or ten students. Regulations *may* require liability insurance, health exams for teachers and students, fire and safety inspections, and health procedures, and may include facility, space, and equipment requirements. Seldom are teachers required to have degrees or courses in early childhood education, and we are aware of no curriculum guides designed for use with preschoolers.

Even if your group is not required to have a license, fire inspection can always be requested, and day care or nursery school licensing standards from your own state can provide a guide to making a safe and healthy environment for your home nursery school. Addresses for each state agency and brief statements of licensing policy at the time of this writing are provided below.

Alabama. No regulations govern nursery schools meeting fewer than four hours a day.

Department of Pensions and Security
Bureau Family and Children's Services
Administrative Building
64 North Union Street
Montgomery, Alabama 36130

Alaska. Nursery schools for seven or more students are licensed according to day-care-center standards. If there are six or fewer students, no license is required.

Department of Health and Social Services
Division of Social Services
Pouch H-05
Juneau, Alaska 99811

Arizona. Nursery schools are licensed according to day-care-center standards. You may care for no more than four children unrelated to you in your home, for which no license is required. New regulations are expected soon.

Department of Health Services
Division of Health Resources
Bureau of Day Care Facilities
State Health Building
Phoenix, Arizona 85007

Arkansas. No regulations govern half-day nursery schools of any description.

Department of Human Services
Division of Social Services
P.O. Box 1437
Little Rock, Arkansas 72203

California. Nursery schools are licensed as day-care centers, but regulations specifically exempt cooperative arrangements between parents where no pay is involved.

Department of Health
Licensing and Certification Division
714 P Street
Sacramento, California 95814

246

Colorado. If you care for five or more children who are not related to you, your nursery school must be licensed according to day-care-center standards. If there are fewer than five unrelated children in your group, no license is required.

Department of Social Services
1575 Sherman Street
Denver, Colorado 80203

Connecticut. Nursery schools are licensed according to day-care-center standards, but cooperative home nursery schools are not regulated.

Department of Health
79 Elm Street
Hartford, Connecticut 06115

Delaware. No regulations govern half-day nursery schools meeting fewer than four hours a day. A voluntary organization of preschool owners and operators has rules for self-regulation: Nursery Kindergarten Association of Delaware, 915 Westover Road, Wilmington, Delaware.

Department of Health and Social Services
Division of Social Services
P.O. Box 309
Wilmington, Delaware 19899

District of Columbia. Nursery schools are licensed according to day-care standards. "Informal parent-supervised neighborhood playgroups" are exempted from regulation.

Department of Human Resources
Licensing and Certification Division
1406 L Street, N.W.
Washington, D.C. 20005

Florida. No uniform statewide standards exist, but nursery schools receiving payment for services are regulated by individual boards of county commissioners if their standards meet or exceed state regulations. Otherwise, a county board may contract with the state Department of Health and Rehabilitative Services to regulate nursery schools according to day-care-center standards. If day care is "regularly provided" to fewer than five children, a "Family Day Care License" is required, but no mention is made of a cooperative home nursery school meeting without payment or compensation.

Department of Health and Rehabilitative Services
1323 Winewood Blvd.
Tallahassee, Florida 32301

Georgia. No license is required for half-day programs not housed in day-care centers. Local building codes and state fire safety codes are applied in some areas.

Department of Human Resources
Child Care Licensing Unit
618 Ponce De Leon Avenue, NE
Atlanta, Georgia 30308

Hawaii. According to rules proposed in March 1978, anyone caring for two or more children for any length of time with or without pay is regulated according to day-care standards. Previous regulations distinguished between "occasional" and "regular" care.

Department of Social Services and Housing
Public Welfare Division
P.O. Box 339
Honolulu, Hawaii 96809

Idaho. No regulations govern half-day nursery schools, but a voluntary day-care "license" may be obtained.

Child Care Coordinator
Department of Health and Welfare
State House
Boise, Idaho 83702

Illinois. Nursery schools for more than eight students are licensed according to day-care-center standards. If your group has eight or fewer students, look into the rules for "Day Care Homes."

Department of Children and Family Services
State Administrative Offices
One North Old State Capitol Plaza
Springfield, Illinois 62706

Indiana. No regulations govern half-day nursery schools of any description.

Department of Public Welfare
Children's Division
Indianapolis, Indiana 46204

Iowa. Nursery schools are licensed under rules for day-care centers if they care for seven or more children for more than two hours a day on a "regular basis." Groups and establishments that provide licensed care for fewer than seven children are called "Family Day Care Homes," but "regular basis" is not clearly defined.

Department of Social Service
State Office Building
Des Moines, Iowa 50319

Kansas. Nursery schools for seven or more children are licensed according to day-care-center standards. If there are six or fewer children, no license is required.

Department of Health and Environment
Bureau of Maternal and Child Health
Topeka, Kansas 66620

Kentucky. Nursery schools are regulated by the Department of Education and the Department of Human Resources. But "a group would not need a license if the children were not cared for in the same home for more than one day of any one week."

Department for Human Resources
Office of Inspector General
Frankfort, Kentucky 40601

Also consult:

State Department of Education

Louisiana. Nursery schools for eight or more children unrelated to the operator are licensed according to day-care standards. If there are seven or fewer children besides your own child, no license is required.

Department of Health and Human Resources
Office of Family Services
755 Riverside North
P.O. Box 44065
Baton Rouge, Louisiana 70804

Maine. There are regulations designed specifically for nursery schools. Buildings must meet standards for "Family Day Care Homes." A home nursery school with three or more children may require licensing if it is considered a "regular program."

Department of Human Services
Social Services Unit
State House
Augusta, Maine 04333

Maryland. There are detailed and specific standards for nursery schools. Since a "school" is defined as any group "offering instruction in any specific place or places," licensing may be required unless your home nursery school meets mainly for the express purpose of "social interaction."

Department of Education
P.O. Box 8717
BWI Airport
Baltimore, Maryland 21240

Massachusetts. Nursery schools are licensed according to day-care-center standards, but the regulations do not cover cooperative arrangements.

Commonwealth of Massachusetts
Office for Children
Day Care Consultation and Licensing
120 Boylston Street
Boston, Massachusetts 02116

For printed matter:

State Book Store
Room 11b
State House
Boston, Massachusetts 02133

Michigan. Under recently proposed regulations, nursery schools for more than six students in a facility other than a private residence will be licensed according to day-care-center standards. These rules are expected to be published by the end of 1978.

Department of Social Services
Bureau of Regulatory Services
300 South Capitol Avenue
Lansing, Michigan 48926

Minnesota. Nursery schools are licensed according to day-care-center standards. Home nursery schools may be subject to licensing as family day care (two to five children), or group day care (six to ten children) "if any parent had more than two children in care for more than 30 days in any calendar year."

Department of Public Welfare
Non-Residential Licensing Section
Centennial Office Building
St. Paul, Minnesota 55155

Mississippi. No regulations govern half-day nursery schools meeting fewer than four hours a day.

Board of Health
P.O. Box 1700
Jackson, Mississippi 39206

Missouri. No regulations govern half-day nursery schools of any description.

Department of Social Services
Division of Family Services
Broadway State Office Building
P.O. Box 88
Jefferson City, Missouri 65101

Montana. No state regulations govern nursery schools, but some local communities have building codes and require fire inspection. New regulations regarding teacher and curriculum standards are to be introduced during the 1979 state legislative session.

Social and Rehabilitation Services
Child and Youth Development Bureau
P.O. Box 4201
Helena, Montana 59601

Nebraska. No regulations govern half-day nursery schools of any description.

Department of Public Welfare
Division of Social Services
Day Care Licensing Consultant
P.O. Box 95026
Lincoln, Nebraska 68509

Nevada. Nursery schools are licensed according to specific preschool standards plus day-care-center standards. If there is no compensation for services, a home nursery school would not require licensing.

Division of Health
Bureau of Health Facilities
Capitol Complex
505 East King Street
Carson City, Nevada 89710

New Hampshire. Nursery schools for seven or more students are licensed according to day-care-center standards. If there are six or fewer children, licensing is not required.

Department of Health and Welfare
Bureau of Child and Family Services
8 London Road
Concord, New Hampshire 03301

New Jersey. Nursery schools for more than five children are licensed according to day-care-center standards. "However, if the children cared for are the same children of the parents within the group, then the licensing law would not apply to such a group."

Department of Human Services
Division of Youth and Family Services
One South Montgomery Street
P.O. Box 510
Trenton, New Jersey 08625

New Mexico. Nursery schools for more than four children are licensed according to day-care-center standards. If there are four or less in the group, regulations do not apply. Changes in policy may occur with future governmental reorganization.

Health and Social Services Department
Social Services Agency
Licensing and Approval Section
P.O. Box 2348
Room 518 PERA Building
Santa Fe, New Mexico 87503

New York. Except in New York City, nursery schools operating two daily sessions of less than three hours each do not require a license. If they provide sessions of three or more hours a day, they are licensed according to day-care standards. The state Education Department registers nursery schools on a voluntary basis. A home nursery school would not be regulated if the children stay for less than three hours. *New York City* regulates all programs operating for five or more hours a week. For more details, contact the City Department of Health, Child Health Bureau, 125 Worth, New York, New York 10013.

> Department of Social Services
> Day Care Licensing Supervisor
> 40 North Pearl Street
> Albany, New York 12243

North Carolina. No regulations govern nursery schools meeting fewer than four hours a day.

> Department of Administration
> Office of Child Day Care Licensing
> P.O. Box 10157
> Raleigh, North Carolina 27605

North Dakota. No regulations govern half-day nursery schools of any description.

> Social Service Board of North Dakota
> Day Care Services Supervisor
> State Capitol
> Bismarck, North Dakota 58505

Ohio. Nursery schools are licensed as "Part-Time Day Care Centers," and must conform to all day-care regulations except for provision of cots for napping. If a home nursery school provides care for fewer than five children besides those of the teaching mother, licensing is not required.

> Department of Public Welfare
> Division of Social Services
> 30 East Broad Street, 30th Floor
> Columbus, Ohio 43215

Oklahoma. No day-care license is required for a nursery school whose purpose is "primarily educational." There is no licensing of family day-care homes for informal, independent arrangements "not on a regular basis, where the care-giver is not compensated, and no advertising is done in any way."

254

Public Welfare Commission
Department of Institutions, Social and Rehabilitative Services
P.O. Box 25352
Oklahoma City, Oklahoma 73125

Oregon. No regulations govern half-day nursery schools meeting less than four hours a day. The state Department of Education registers preschools with more than one grade level on a voluntary basis.

Department of Human Resources
Children's Services Division
198 Commercial Street
Salem, Oregon 97310

For voluntary registration:

Department of Education
942 Lancaster Drive, N.E.
Salem, Oregon 97310

Pennsylvania. Nursery schools are under the jurisdiction of the Department of Education. "Any difficult or unusual situation" will be resolved jointly by the Department of Education and the Department of Public Welfare. Child care programs providing care for fewer than four hours at a time on an intermittent basis are covered under "drop-in" care.

Department of Public Welfare
Bureau of Child Care and Development
Health and Welfare Building, Room 423
Harrisburg, Pennsylvania 17120

Rhode Island. The Department of Education provides specific, clear, and complete regulations for nursery schools, but no mention is made in these rules of a home nursery school situation.

Department of Education
199 Promenade Street
Providence, Rhode Island 02908

255

South Carolina. No regulations govern half-day nursery schools of any description.

>Department of Social Services
>Office of Child Development
>P.O. Box 1520
>Columbia, South Carolina 29202

South Dakota. Nursery schools must meet fire and safety standards for their buildings and may conform to other standards on a voluntary basis. A cooperative home nursery school would not require licensing.

>Department of Educational and Cultural Affairs
>Division of Elementary and Secondary Education
>State Capitol Building
>Pierre, South Dakota 57501

Tennessee. Nursery schools are licensed according to day-care-center standards if they enroll thirteen or more children. According to day-care regulations, a person receiving pay for care of five to seven children requires a "Family Day Care" license, but if care is provided for fewer than five children not related to the operator, no license is required.

>Department of Human Services
>Licensing Unit
>410 State Office Building
>Nashville, Tennessee 37219

Texas. Nursery school requirements are extensive and specifically adapted to the nursery school situation. For a cooperative home nursery school, "such an arrangement would likely be subject to our requirements for Registered Family Homes, Group Day Care Homes, or Family Day Care Homes."

>Department of Public Welfare
>Department of Human Resources
>Day Care Licensing
>John H. Reagan Building
>Austin, Texas 78701

Utah. No state regulations govern nursery schools meeting less than four hours a day. If your nursery school is a business, however, you should have fire and sanitation clearance and a business license.

Department of Social Services
Division of Family Services
150 West North Temple, Room 370
P.O. Box 2500
Salt Lake City, Utah 84110

Vermont. Nursery schools are licensed as "Early Childhood Facilities." Specific safety standards are required for nursery school facilities. A home nursery school may be considered an Early Childhood Facility if it provides service on a "regular or continual basis."

Department of Social and Rehabilitative Services
Social Services Division
Licensing and Regulations Unit
State Office Building
Montpelier, Vermont 05602

Virginia. No regulations govern half-day nursery schools meeting fewer than four hours a day.

Department of Welfare
Division of Licensing
Bureau of Standards, Policy, Manual and Training
Blair Building
8007 Discovery Drive
Richmond, Virginia 23288

Washington. No regulations govern half-day nursery schools meeting fewer than four hours a day.

Department of Social and Health Services
Child Care Agencies Unit
Olympia, Washington 98504

West Virginia. Nursery schools are not licensed, but must meet fire and health standards, according to the state Fire Commission. Parents with a home nursery school should also contact the Fire Commission.

Department of Welfare
State Office Building No. 6
Charleston, West Virginia 25305

For fire and health standards:

Fire Commission
1800 Washington Street, East
Charleston, West Virginia 25305

Wisconsin. Nursery schools are covered under present licensing regulations, but a "total revision" is expected because the Department of Social Services is being completely reorganized. One prepared revision would allow cooperative groups to exist without a license if no compensation were given in the form of cash, gifts, or other services. A cooperative home nursery school as described in this book would qualify for this exemption.

Department of Health and Social Services
Division of Community Services
Bureau of Alternate Care
1 Wilson Street
Madison, Wisconsin 53702

Wyoming. Nursery schools must meet guidelines for "educational facilities" as well as conform to day-care-center rules. Home nursery schools are exempted as "cooperative exchanges." The rules are presently being revised.

Department of Health and Social Services
Division of Public Assistance and Social Services
Hathaway Building
Cheyenne, Wyoming 82002

Bibliography

Early Childhood Development and Training

Ames, Louise, and Joan Ames Chase. *Don't Push Your Preschooler.* New York: Harper and Row, 1974.

Beck, Helen L. *Don't Push Me, I'm No Computer.* New York: McGraw-Hill, 1973.

Goodlad, John. *Early Schooling in the United States.* New York: McGraw-Hill, 1973.

Landreth, Catherine. *Preschool Learning and Teaching.* New York: Harper and Row, 1972.

Leeper, Sarah *et al. Good Schools for Young Children, A Guide for Working With Three-, Four-, and Five-Year-Olds.* Second Edition. New York: Macmillan, 1968.

Neisser, Edith G. *Primer for Parents of Preschoolers.* New York: Parents' Magazine Press, 1972.

Pitcher, Evelyn G., *et al. Helping Young Children Learn.* Columbus, Oh.: Merrill, 1966.

Read, Katherine H. *The Nursery School: A Human Relations Laboratory.* Fourth Edition. Philadelphia: Saunders, 1966.

Roufberg, Ruth B. *Today He Can't, Tomorrow He Can! Your Child from Two to Five Years: A Comprehensive Guide to Educational Materials.* New York: Fountain, 1971.

Todd, Vivian and Helen Hefferman. *The Years Before School.* New York: Macmillan, 1970.

Watts, Harriett. *How to Start Your Own Preschool Playgroup.* New York: Universe, 1973.

Winick, Mariann P. *Before the 3 Rs.* New York: McKay, 1973.

Health and Safety

Chinn, Peggy L. *Child Health Maintenance: Concepts in Family Centered Care.* St. Louis: Mosby, 1975.

Creese, Angela. *Safety for Your Family.* New York: International Publication Service, 1968.

Feinbloom, Richard. *Child Health Encyclopedia: A Complete Guide for Parents.* New York: Delta, 1975.

Green, Martin I. *A Sigh of Relief: The First-Aid Handbook for Childhood Emergencies.* New York: Bantam, 1977.

Isbister, Clair. *Mommy, I Feel Sick.* New York: Hawthorn, 1978.

Schulz, Gene C. "How to Poison-Proof Your Home." *Parents' Magazine,* May 1977.

Vickery, Donald M. and James F. Fries. *Take Care of Yourself: A Consumers Guide to Medical Care.* Menlo Park, Calif.: Addison-Wesley, 1976.

Songs and Fingerplay

Bramblett, Ella. *Shoots of Green: Poems for Young Gardeners.* New York: Crowell, 1968.

Grayson, Marion. *Let's Do Fingerplays.* Washington, D.C.: Luce, 1962.

Helfman, Harry. *Fun With Your Fingers.* New York: Morrow, 1968.

Hogstrom, Daphne. *My Big Book of Finger Plays.* Racine, Wisc.: Western, 1974.

Jacobs, Frances E. *Finger Plays and Action Rhymes.* New York: Lothrop, Lee and Shepard, 1961.

Le Bar, Mary. *Activity Music for 4's and 5's.* Wheaton, Ill.: Scripture Press, 1960.

Paulsson, Emilie. *Finger Plays for Nursery and Kindergarten.* New York: Lothrop, Lee and Shepard, 1963.

Scott, Louise and J. J. Thompson. *Rhymes for Fingers and Flannelboards.* St. Louis: McGraw-Hill, 1960.

Seeger, Ruth C. *American Folk Songs for Children.* Garden City, N.Y.: Doubleday, 1948.

Preschool Craft Ideas

Clapper, Edna and John. *Pack-O-Fun: Make it From Odds 'n Ends.* New York: Hawthorn, 1973.

Clapper, Edna and John. *Pack-O-Fun: Treasury of Craft, Gifts, and Toys.* New York: Hawthorn, 1971.

D'Amato, Janet and Alex. *Cardboard Carpentry.* New York: Lion, 1966.

Gilbreath, Alice. *Spouts, Lids, and Cans.* New York: Morrow, 1973.

Gilbreath, Alice. *Beginning Crafts for Beginning Readers.* Chicago: Follett, 1972.

Lamarque, Colette. *The Fun-to-Make Book.* New York: Golden, 1970.

Lapshire, Robert. *How to Make Flibbers, Etc.* New York: Random House, 1964.

Leeming, Joseph. *Papercraft: How to Make Toys, Favors and Useful Articles.* New York: Lippincott, 1949.

Mandry, Kathy and Joe Tato. *How to Grow a Jelly Glass Farm.* New York: Pantheon, 1974.

McNeice, William. *Crafts for Retarded.* Bloomington, Ill.: McNight and McNight, 1964.

Nagle, Avery and Joseph Leeming. *Kitchen Table Fun.* New York: Lippincott, 1961.

Newsome, Arden. *Cork and Wood Crafts.* New York: Lion, 1970.

Pflug, Betsy. *Pint-Size Fun.* New York: Lippincott, 1972.

Razzi, James. *Just For Kids!* New York: Parents' Magazine Press, 1974.

Sattler, Helen Roney. *Kitchen Carton Crafts.* New York: Lothrop, Lee and Shepard, 1970.

Seidelman, James and Grace Mintonye. *Creating with Papier Mâché.* New York: Crowell-Collier, 1971.

Slake, Richard. *Carton Craft.* New York: Phillips, 1972.

Miscellaneous Activities

Alhouse, Rosemary and Cecil Main, Jr. *Science Experiences for*

Young Children. New York: Columbia University Teachers' College Press, 1975.

Chambers, Wicke and Spring Asher. *The Lip-Smackin' Joke-Crackin' Cookbook for Kids.* New York: Golden, 1975.

Cherry, Clare. *Creative Art for the Developing Child.* Belmont, Calif.: Fearon, 1972.

Cherry, Clare. *Creative Movement.* Belmont, Calif.: Fearon, 1972.

Croft, Doreen J. and Robert D. Hess. *An Activities Handbook for Teachers of Young Children.* Boston: Houghton Mifflin, 1972.

Dorian, Margery and Francis Gulland. *Tell Stories Through Movement.* Belmont, Calif.: Fearon, n.d.

Durland, Frances C. *Creative Dramatics for Children.* Yellow Springs, Oh.: Antioch, 1952.

Geri, Frank. *Games and Rhythms for Children.* New York: Prentice-Hall, 1955.

Hamlin, Alice P. *Singing Games for Children.* Cincinnati: Willis Music, n.d.

Harrell, Donna and Wesley Haystead. *Creative Bible Learning for Young Children, Birth to 5 Years.* Glendale, Calif.: Regal, 1977.

Hartley, Ruth and Robert Goldenson. *The Complete Book of Children's Play.* New York: Crowell, 1963.

Hein, Lucille. *Entertaining Your Child.* New York: Harper and Row, 1971.

Helfman, Harry. *Making Pictures Move.* New York: Morrow, 1969.

Jordan, Diana. *Childhood and Movement.* Oxford: Basil Blackwell, 1972.

Kellogg, Rhoda. *The How of Successful Finger Painting.* Palo Alto, Calif.: Fearon, 1958.

Kranzer, Herman C. *Nursery and Kindergarten Science Activities.* Jenkintown, Penn.: Baker, 1967.

Sattler, Helen Roney. *Recipes for Art and Craft Material.* New York: Lothrop, Lee and Shepard, 1973.

Self, Margaret. *202 Things to Do: Activities and Finger Fun for Children.* Glendale, Calif.: Regal, 1968.

Siks, Geraldine B. *Creative Dramatics, An Art for Children.* New York: Harper and Row, 1958.

Index

Notes

Notes

Notes

Notes

Notes

Notes

Notes